The Challenge of the Market: Privatization and Publishing in Africa

BELLAGIO STUDIES IN PUBLISHING
Philip G. Altbach, General Editor

Other titles in this series include:

1: Philip G. Altbach, editor, *Publishing in Africa and the Third World*

2: Carol Priestley, *Publishing Assistance Programs: Review and Inventory*

3: Philip G. Altbach and Hyaeweol Choi, *Bibliography on Publishing in the Third World, 1980-1993* (Published by Ablex Publishers, 355 Chestnut St., Norwood, NJ 07648 USA)

4: Philip G. Altbach, editor, *Copyright and Development: Inequality in the Information Age*

5: Urvashi Butalia and Ritu Menon, *Making a Difference: Feminist Publishing in the South*

6: Henry M. Chakava, *Publishing in Africa: One Man's Perspective* (Copublished with East African Educational Publishers, Ltd., Nairobi)

The Challenge of the Market: *Privatization and Publishing in Africa*

Philip G. Altbach, editor

Bellagio Studies in Publishing, 7

Bellagio Publishing Network
Research and Information Center
in association with the Boston College
Center for International Higher Education

August 1996

Bellagio Studies in Publishing publications are distributed by the African Books Collective, Ltd.

© 1996 Bellagio Publishing Network

Copies of this book may be ordered from
African Books Collective, Ltd.
The Jam Factory
27 Park End St.
Oxford OX1 1HU, UK
Fax: 44-1865-793298

ISBN: 0964-6078-2-4

Bellagio Studies in Publishing, 7

TABLE OF CONTENTS

Introduction	1
1. Perspectives on Privatization in African Publishing Philip G. Altbach	3
2. The Transition from State to Commercial Publishing Systems in African Countries Paul Brickhill	9
3. The Transition to Privatization in Publishing: Ghana's Experience Richard A. B. Crabbe	29
4. Privatization and the Challenges for Publishing in Ethiopia Atnafu Wassie	47
5. Privatization in Publishing: The Zambian Experience Ray Munamwimbu	63
6. Privatization of Publishing in the Côte d'Ivoire Robert J. Palmeri	79
7. Transition or Collapse? A Survey of the Prospects for Private Publishing in Central Asia Pernille Askerud	95
Contributors	113

INTRODUCTION

The topic for this book was suggested by Atnafu Wassie, one of our contributors, at a seminar sponsored by the Bellagio Publishing Network and APNET in Addis Ababa, Ethiopia about a year ago. Privatization, Wassie noted, was around the corner in Ethiopia, and much could be learned from the experience of other countries. In order to further our understanding of the experience of privatization in publishing, we asked colleagues working in several African countries to reflect on the experience in their areas. For a contrast, we have included a chapter concerning the central Asian republics of the former Soviet Union. We begin with two overview evaluations which point out that the road to privatization is not necessarily an easy one, and that there are costs as well as benefits involved. Our case studies, from different African regions, point to specific experiences.

We are indebted to Atnafu Wassie for the idea, and to our contributors for taking the time to reflect on their experiences. All of the African contributors are themselves publishers, who bring to their essays experience as well as reflections. The work of the Research and Information Center of the Bellagio Publishing Network is supported by the Rockefeller Foundation, and is a part of the activities of the Center for International Higher Education at Boston College. Edith Hoshino and Liz Reisberg helped with the editing. James JF Forest assisted with the design and layout.

Philip G. Altbach
Chestnut Hill, Massachusetts

1
Perspectives on Privatization in African Publishing

PHILIP G. ALTBACH

Privatization is the slogan of the decade. A combination of forces has brought it to center stage. The collapse of the Soviet Union and the ideology of state socialism, the failure of state enterprises in many countries, the dominant ideology of the World Bank and other foreign assistance agencies, and the lack of funds available from governmental sources all impel privatization initiatives. African publishing has been significantly affected by the privatization movement. Few would argue that the earlier efforts to build state-run or parastatal publishing enterprises have been successful. Indeed, the experience has been a near universal failure.

State-run publishers have exhibited a powerful combination of negative characteristics. These include the following:
- poor management based on the civil service model, with a lack of accountability for results, failure to understand market forces, lack of incentives to meet demand, and related problems. This led to slow production, inadequate control of costs, and general inefficiency;
- corruption, where endemic in the government, often extending to public enterprises—including publishing;
- lack of capital for purchasing machinery, paper, technology, etc.;
- lack of understanding of the special circumstances of publishing;
- close ties to ruling groups and parties, and a related unwillingness to publish books free of political or ideological considerations; and
- monopolization of and dependence on the textbook market, and lack of attention to any other element of publishing.

The ideas that led to state publishing now seem mistaken, but they were powerful forces in the 1960s, when these agencies were for the most part established. It should be kept in mind that there was virtually no private capital available to establishing a publishing industry, and the few entrepreneurs who existed were more interested in investments with prospects for quicker returns than publishing can provide even under the best of circumstances. There was also an urgent need to provide indigenous textbooks to a rapidly expanding population of children in schools, and policymakers generally chose what they felt would be the quickest way of producing books—direct government production. It was also assumed that textbooks could be published most cheaply by the public sector and distributed either free or at low cost by education ministries. A pervading belief that the public sector would be the most efficient and effective motor for development, providing both the skills needed and a more egalitarian approach, dominated the thinking of many development experts as well as newly independent governments. Further, governments often felt that private-sector publishers were simply oriented to quick profits and would not be able or inclined to provide books, especially textbooks, at a reasonable price and with good production standards.

Socialist ideas were popular, and many of the regimes established after independence had socialist ideas or sympathies. It was not only the newly independent African governments that held to this view. Foreign assistance agencies and multinational lenders such as the World Bank also preferred to deal with governments rather than private entrepreneurs. It is important to keep in mind the context—economic, political, and policy—that existed when public-sector publishing was established. Even many multinational publishers, such as British-based Macmillans, favored working with government publishers in order to dominate markets.

Indigenous publishing does not have deep historical roots in Africa, and circumstances during the colonial era and its immediate aftermath did not favor it. During the colonial period, books were imported from the colonizing power, and there were few efforts to produce books locally. Indeed, some colonizers, most notably the French, felt that producing books in the metropole was the best policy. Book exports from the metropole not only ensured that the ideas made available to the colonized were acceptable to the colonizers, but also provided a small advantage to the metropolitan publishers. Where local publishers existed, they were often branches of large firms from the metropole. This was the most common British approach to the provision of books in their colonies. In some countries, there was a small publishing base that was implanted by Christian missionary organizations. In no sub-Saharan African nation, with the exception of South Africa, was there a functioning book industry at the time of independence. The only partial exceptions to this generalization are Kenya and Nigeria.

Public-sector publishing has, by and large, failed, although in many countries the record is mixed. State enterprises were often able to take the textbooks designed by ministries of education and design and print books for the schools fairly quickly. These books were often poorly produced and sometimes too expensive, but at least they provided indigenous material to school students. In many countries, public-sector publishers were the first publishers to be established in a context where there was little expertise concerning book publishing. In short, the circumstances surrounding the growth of publishing in Africa were not favorable, and it is not surprising that success proved to be elusive. It is an open question whether private enterprise could have done better under the quite difficult circumstances that prevailed at the time—and to some extent still prevail today.

Private-sector publishing faces some daunting challenges in the contemporary African context. It is worth discussing some in an effort to understand the economic, political, and practical issues. It is certainly insufficient simply to point to the shortcomings of past public-sector efforts without providing a context in which private initiative may flourish.

- Public policy. Private publishing operates in the context of governmental policy. This is true in any country, but it is even more important in Africa, where circumstances must be favorable for the success of any new enterprise because of the difficult economic climate. So far, with very few exceptions, governmental policy has negatively affected publishing. Lack of recognition of publishing as a strategic industry, tariff barriers, high taxes, and other restrictions have marked public policy. For private-sector publishing to flourish, the government must provide a favorable climate. Tax structures set up to foster publishing and book distribution, recognition of publishing as an important part of the economy, access without tariffs to needed imported materials (such as paper, computers, supplies and the like), a trade regime that permits the import and export of books, and other initiatives are necessary elements of a coherent set of governmental policies aimed at supporting an indigenous and independent publishing industry. It is the case that even when pronouncements have been made, sometimes through national book development councils or other government-publisher forums, little has been done in terms of policy. Successful private publishing must have a favorable environment in which to operate.

- Freedom to publish. Often ignored in discussions of book development is the importance of an atmosphere of freedom in which to publish. Censorship, intimidation, and restrictions on the freedom to publish will necessarily hinder the emergence of a vibrant publishing industry. Governments must permit private-sector publishers to operate without intellectual restrictions.
- Access to credit. One of the greatest problems for publishers in developing countries is the lack of financing for book publishing. In the West, even in the best of circumstances, publishing is seldom highly profitable. In Africa, return on investment is slow at best, but when interest rates are 25 percent or more, successful publishing is very difficult. It is not surprising that scarce capital will flow to industries that offer a better return. A further problem is that neither the government nor the banks consider publishing to be an "industry," and this eliminates access to some kinds of credit. Publishing must have access to credit on favorable terms if it is to survive. It must be said, however, that in some cases indigenous publishers have not operated in a way that gave confidence to lenders, thus making it even more difficult for the book industry to raise needed capital.
- Size. The simple fact is that in most African nations the current market for books is tiny, and even with improvements in literacy and purchasing power, markets will remain small. It is, of course, difficult to establish a viable publishing industry in small markets. But it is not impossible. Policies and practices that encourage publishing in small markets need to be developed. For example, new technologies permit "short-run" books to be profitable—but the cost of these technologies is high.
- The multinationals. As literacy grows and economies pick up, the potential market for books increases in Africa. Western multinational publishers did not see Africa as a major market for expansion, although some, notably British firms, were involved even during the period of public-sector dominance, often in collaboration with state-run publishers. When economic problems loomed, these multinationals scaled back their involvement or even left, causing additional difficulties for the provision of books. Now, with the growth of a private sector and with improving economic circumstances, multinational publishers are beginning to be attracted to the emerging African markets. A further issue is the potential role of large South African publishers, excluded from most African countries during the apartheid regime, but currently active in several countries. Local indigenous firms will find it difficult

to compete with the multinationals, which have access to capital, expertise and distribution. Means must be found to encourage indigenous firms to flourish, while at the same permitting access to the multinationals.
- Partnerships and collaboration. Much has been said about partnerships between indigenous African publishers and multinationals, with other Northern publishers, or among African publishers. Fostering such partnerships can be an important part of publishing development in Africa. There are, however, serious issues involved, such as financial arrangements, control, and marketing. All too often, idealistic notions of partnership become domination by the wealthier and more experienced partner.
- Textbooks. Textbooks are the largest single part of publishing in any developing country, and in some countries, they are virtually the only viable part of the publishing industry. In many parts of Africa, textbooks have been produced by government agencies or imported from abroad. Private-sector publishers should be entitled to a significant share of the lucrative textbook market. For many years, textbooks will be the largest single element of publishing—private firms need to have access to textbook production.
- The World Bank and aid agencies. Multilateral and bilateral lending and assistance agencies have long been active in Africa. A small number have been concerned about book development, and several, especially the World Bank, have been involved in publishing through supporting the publication of textbooks. Because of the small size and weak infrastructures of indigenous publishers, these foreign agencies may assume a large role in publishing. The World Bank, especially, has lent large sums for textbook development and publication. Most Bank-supported programs have not helped indigenous private firms, despite the Bank's ostensible commitment to the private sector. Indeed, some have argued that Bank textbook programs have actually weakened private publishers by eliminating the most lucrative part of the book market. The World Bank and assistance agencies must orient their policies toward assisting the emerging private-sector publishing industry.
- Intra-African book trade. Currently, it is very difficult for African-published books to be sold within Africa. Problems of currency convertibility, poor transportation networks, weak distribution channels, and other obstacles hinder the intra-African book trade. It is important to build up the structures that can foster this trade.

These and other elements are central to understanding the potential for successful private-sector publishing in Africa. It is necessary first to comprehend the factors involved before policies and practices can be put into place that will ensure success. It is hoped that the book sector can build on a thorough understanding of the issues.

2

The Transition from State to Commercial Publishing Systems in African Countries

PAUL BRICKHILL

This chapter offers insight into the problems and issues in the transition from state to private textbook supply, underway in several African countries. The conclusions are based on studies I have done in Tanzania, Zambia, and Malawi, and observations and discussions with publishers from Mozambique, Ethiopia, Ghana and Kenya. Zimbabwe, where my main experience lies, has a private system of textbook provision and provided a useful reference for transitions elsewhere. In revisiting documents, I find that my views have remained largely unchanged, albeit tempered by discussions with African publishers. I hope this paper provokes as much as it informs.

Introduction
    I would be a little suspicious of anyone described as an authority on the vexing question of the transition from state to commercial book provision. There are too many factors specific to one country, not least among them the economic and political terrain in which the process takes place. The real experts are the practitioners—publishers, booksellers, and educators grappling with practical day-to-day problems. Nor am I convinced that rapid transition to a free market system alone offers the sole and unequivocal route to vibrant national book provision without regard for circumstances. In poor countries, poor people cannot afford books. Most African countries arrived at independence with little or no publishing infrastructure, compelling state intervention. Realistically, commercialization has to be accompanied by a national book policy to secure the "national character" of publishing, the needs of readers (for example, language policy), and all the components of the book chain, from authorship to distribution.
    To pose the question, as one hears on occasion from enthusiastic advocates of private enterprise, only in terms of one system or the other is simplistic. If the transition is not understood as a long-term, ongo-

ing process in the national interest, to be supported until all components of the "book chain" function, failure is likely to be repeated. There is no quick fix. Book development demands long-term planning. Certain patterns are quite evident in this transition and common problems are emerging. It is these I wish draw out and highlight.

The Background to State Intervention
State intervention in the book sector at the dawn of African independence was not as irrational as it appears today in the era of free market economics. It was a widely appealing concept in African nationalist political circles. It was seriously considered even in postindependent Zimbabwe as late as the mid-1980s, despite Zimbabwe's strong commercial publishing and bookselling base.

The main ingredient to state intervention was control over the textbook publishing industry, brought about by imposing a state monopoly to provide sufficient, appropriate, inexpensive (or free) textbooks for schools, invariably coupled with a new African-centered curriculum. Education was a highly charged political issue in postcolonial Africa. To most Africans, colonial education had been a "tool of the oppressor." Having been denied access to equal (or any) education in the past except in a few mission schools, many Africans felt they had been "educated" to perpetuate colonial rule and subjected to insidious anti-African attitudes in textbooks. On independence, nation building meant correcting the injustices of the past. The hunger for education was overwhelming in all of the new African states. Politically, education had to serve the needs of "the people," where the inherited system had been designed to exclude this. Expectations were fiercely high that education would "deliver" a new generation from poverty and oppression.

How was the textbook provision mechanism to function? There was overwhelming dependence on foreign authors and imported materials tied to the examination systems and curriculum of the former colonial power. Newly independent African countries had virtually no indigenous publishing capacity, outside of religious materials. Where subsidiaries of foreign publishers existed they exercised a monopoly over textbook provision, based largely on importing books from their parent company and sometimes reprinting these locally. The Lusophone and most Francophone countries had no publishing or printing infrastructure.

The State Provider Mentality

Against this background and the needs of rapidly expanding education systems and new curriculums, it was expected and, indeed, responsible for the state to turn provider. The long-term prospects for an indigenous, commercial book sector were not apparent then. The economics of publishing, as an industry, was not understood because there was hardly a publishing industry. What was required, quickly, were large quantities of cheap or free textbooks, devised or adapted for local conditions, which only the state could provide. State intervention was not seen as merely an interim phase in a larger context of national book development.

The "state provider" mentality, became entrenched in the popular psyche in a few years and is now difficult to dislodge. As state textbook provision systems developed over the years, funded extensively by donors, the mentality strengthened and the possibility of changing course grew more distant. The number of education ministry employees deriving their livelihood from state publishing grew, a bureaucracy of textbook provision grew, adherents grew, and the budget grew. The system justified itself. The budgets, unconstrained by profit and loss considerations, rationalized by the growing shortage of textbooks, grew steadily.

Arguments have been constructed over the years, in different settings, to justify continued state monopoly over textbook provision, even as it entered crisis. The alternative, where no indigenous publishing industry had emerged, seemed to be dependence on foreign books. Ironically, the fact that there was no indigenous commercial publishing or book trade capacity—may have been itself an outcome of the state monopoly. Where local commercial publishers were established, the argument against business interests "profiteering from the education of children" has been put forward. This view can still be heard, faintly, in dusty corridors in many education ministries.

These arguments and those with a socialist ideological slant (central planning, state ownership of the means of production) are secondary to the state-provider mentality. Whatever its initial intentions, it came to reinforce party control and the politics of patronage, which became in the broader context, an overriding issue in African politics.

The Lack of Policy

The lethargy in developing mechanisms for book provision

throughout Africa is effected by the lack of national data and policies related to culture in general, let alone book policies. African governments consistently refuse to pay serious attention to the chorus of independent media and cultural professionals saying that information is a strategic national industry and resource. As is the case in other strategic areas, it must be allowed to grow and function, secured by a sound conceptual framework, policy instruments, and, ideally, legislation.

African governments have not listened to their own publishing professionals. They have listened instead to their employees and (where aid was concerned) to project consultants, few of whom will advise African governments to follow, or even investigate, international developments. Africa is typically regarded as unique and requiring different solutions.

How does Europe, for example, maintain its level and diversity of book output? Even a cursory examination reveals a history of indirect and direct support to national private publishing industries and of profound respect accorded to authors and a culture of literary. The methods are innovative, diverse, and sophisticated, from buy-back systems, research and publishing subsidies, and institutional support for writers and publishers (to strengthen the national language), to incentives to export. The weaker the industry (as in the case of smaller European countries with an insular national language) the greater the level of direct state support. The challenges to successful commercial publishing are not so different between continents.

Publishing is an activity that justifies support everywhere because it results in immense cultural, political, and economic advantages. Consider against this background the almost universal lack of political will throughout Africa even to keep a minimum public library system operating. Lack of funds? We all know about the debts and deficits of African governments, but the amounts required are small even in the tiny national budgets of African governments. Incentives that do not strain public funds are hardly considered. Books and publishing issues, especially in private hands, suffer from neglect and sometimes hostility.

If publishing can be likened to an "ideas factory," the true extent of damage inflicted by government neglect of books as a strategic industry in Africa can begin to be appreciated. An idea is born—technical, social, creative, or otherwise—and the publishing process transforms it into a definite and digestible form and disseminates it. There are, of course, other media channels, but none quite with the durability of the book. Books are read and reread, change hands, and require no technology to use. If flow of information is a direct and essential catalyst to social development, then government disincentives to publishing have stifled nation building in a far broader sense than "textbook provision." They have undermined the capacity to generate, shape, and share ideas. A generation of African thinkers and innovators have been in wasteland. Globally, Africa barely accounts for 1 percent of new book titles. What society can afford this?

Finally, in many African countries national interest has been subordinated to the politics of party and individual patronage too often. That this is not stated openly is central to our problem.

Some Effects of State Control

State subsidies and incentives to a strategic, commercial industry are clearly not the same as state control. One effect of state control in Africa has been to cripple nontextbook publishing. By taking the monopoly on textbooks, the profitable "rump" of publishing, the state has denied private publishers the possibilities of subsidizing a general list with textbook sales.

A equivalent scenario exists with booksellers. To remove booksellers from textbook provision in Africa is to eliminate them and with them their expertise and services.

Henry Chakava has aptly indicated that publishing is a "hands-on activity. It is a personalized trade that thrives best in the hands of individuals," as examples throughout the world confirm. Publishing and publishing industries depend on diversity of expertise. The relative health of any publishing industry can be accurately gauged by its level of diversity. For economic reasons, and particularly in Africa, this diversity can only develop in combination with access to the largest educational markets. Viability is the bottom line.

The importance of supplementary books and a significant number of authors are often mentioned in book studies. Supplementary books are generally published in situations where they can be combined with educational publishing. A truly competitive publishing industry, where state policy supports diversity and free markets, will encourage book diversity as well as a growing pool of specialized authors.

The publishing industry is inherently as broad and diverse as society, and to succeed, it has to move as quickly as society. It is an accepted practice (in large publishers as well as small) that individuals take a publication from concept or manuscript to finished product. Publishing by committees, bureaucracies, and government departments is a caricature of real publishing.

Yet, despite the overwhelming evidence of the inability of state monopolies to sustain minimum book provision, there are success stories. Mozambique—one of Africa's poorest countries, wracked by civil war through the 1980s—produced more than 700 nontextbook titles from 1976 to 1989 in print runs ranging from 3,000 to 20,000. It is hard to see how this output could have been matched by a private sector, even if one had existed. Prior to the emergence of private publishers in the 1970s and 1980s, Ghana provided its primary school pupils with textbooks through state publishing, as did Zambia until economic pressures overwhelmed the country in the 1980s. With an economy based on state ownership, Tanzania had achieved an unprecedented degree of national literacy by the 1970s.

As much as publishing is a "hands-on" process, it also works within the parameters of economy of scale. Large economies of scale in publishing are more productive and cost efficient. This was the relative advantage of state publishing, particularly given the weakness, lack of financing, and inexperience in the private sector.

What therefore makes state publishing bad per se? First, there is a point in the development of economic infrastructure generally, and printing and publishing specifically, at which the capacity of the nation to provide books, independent of the state, exceeds the state's capacity. Where the state continues to cling to its monopoly, it retards publishing development. Book provision depends on the state's productivity, which (when properly managed) can have quite impressive results, can never match the potential of the private sector. Second, monopolies in publishing rarely do more than provide basics and have a tendency toward wastage and inefficiency. The producer is not directly affected by the results in the way compelled by competition.

The Transition to Liberalization

The economic stagnation and crisis throughout Africa in the 1980s forced most African governments and their donors to reconsider their priorities. It is worth remembering that most state monopolies in publishing had become dependent on foreign aid by the 1980s. Governments did not have the money to sustain state textbook provision without it. Donors cannot excuse themselves entirely from the problems of state publishing, since in many cases they paid for it. It is not difficult to understand, despite some protestations to the contrary, that donors have had considerable influence over African book provision. As long as the money was available, few hard-pressed African governments were going to refuse it or the development approaches that went with it. The arrangement seemed to suit both government and donor.

In education development, since the 1970s and throughout the 1980s, the World Bank and major bilateral donors worked as a matter of policy with governments. While some contact was established with private publishers and nongovernmental organizations (NGOs)—by, for instance, Scandinavian donors—typically these were confined to the "cultural desk" or the resident in-country mission. From the early 1990s, the Bellagio Publishing Network has provided a forum for such contacts.

The World Bank had minimal contact with African publishers where education projects were designed in the 1980s, but on the whole the involvement of independent African publishing professionals has been absent from book provision projects. This left development professionals and government education planners to work out the mechanics of textbook provision systems, neither of which had much professional or commercial publishing experience. Thus, foreign consultants were used extensively to provide technical input, but many lacked a real or long-term grounding in African conditions. Mistakes were inevitable.

In November 1993, the African Publishers' Network (APNET) dispatched its chairman, treasurer, executive secretary, and a well-known Tanzanian publisher to Washington, to introduce indigenous African publishing to World Bank officials and seek a reaction. It became clear from this mission and further contact that most World Bank officials, with one or two exceptions, were unaware of the extent, activities, and emergence of an indigenous commercial sector in African publishing—hardly news, by 1993, in African book circles. Moreover, it was apparent that some input, or lobbying, on key questions of African book provision was being provided, directly and indirectly, by British and French multinational publishers.

It was entirely inappropriate that a major body of expertise in commercial publishing—indigenous publishers—hardly featured in the initial thinking about the privatization of African textbook provision. Yet, they held first-hand experience of commercial publishing in Africa, the nascent African book market, its perils, and its potential.

The first error in the privatization of African publishing was the failure to create what Chakava has referred to as a triangular partnership—donor, government, and African publishing professionals—as opposed to a vertical relationship. What forestalled this, partly, was the need to approach privatization regionally, (since African expertise tends to be concentrated in a few publishing centers) and the passive "wait and see" attitude of many African publishers, busy just keeping afloat.

All this is a pity, as African publishers and booksellers not only had the day-to-day experience, they were in many cases further in their thinking than governments and donors about how commercial African textbook provision might work. It is crucial that these shortcomings are now being rectified, both as African publishing organizes itself regionally, through APNET, and by the Association for the Development of African Education (DAE) Working Group in Books and Library Materials (grouping donors to African education), which recognizes APNET as its African partner. Increasingly, but not yet consistently, African publishers are at least being consulted.

The move to break up state monopolies and liberalize was in the first instance the decision of donors, not governments. Elsewhere studies have traced the specific factors that stimulated the "new thinking" to the late 1980s. Clearly, the decisions applied by the major donors to African book provision were mirrored in most other sectors, reflecting the new wave of economic liberalism.

A key point was reached by the time of the 1991 Manchester conference on African textbook provision (where African publishers were minimally represented). After a decade of steadily increasing aid inflows to African education, donors seemed to have reached broad consensus that, in the long term, state monopoly textbook provision was futile. It had failed. The African education ministers and officials present were left with few illusions that change was imminent and necessary. Differences seemed to arise over the method of effecting the transition and whether a fast-track approach was preferable to gradual change.

The Breakdown in Control
Excessive state dependence on donor support had produced debilitating effects on textbook provision. Wastage and inefficiency had become evident throughout state systems. A well-intentioned but nevertheless stifling bureaucracy maintained a monopoly over the publication and distribution of textbooks with donor support and had simply strained all the linkages in the "book chain" to breaking point. Governments embarking on the transition to commercial textbook provision have done so because donor-supported state mechanisms failed to ensure an adequate and sustained supply of textbooks to schools.

Of course, a host of factors came into play in each country, but the breakdown in control is a common theme. Corruption may be too strong a word, but the fact remains that productivity, defined loosely as the number of books reaching pupils' desks against total resources, was declining steadily as economic conditions deteriorated. It is fair to say that some individuals in the state system were corrupt in a petty sense, perhaps influenced by an unremittingly harsh economic background. The job stopped being done properly when families could not be fed. To compound matters, wastage and inefficiency in the state system placed enormous burdens on the dwindling resources needed to keep the system going.

The critical weakness and main reason why control ultimately broke down as conditions deteriorated was that decisions, performance, and results did not directly affect the large number of people engaged in textbook production and supply. This lack of control or accountability in the state systems is well illustrated by the absence of reliable figures, and sometimes even estimates, of basic book data. For example, average pupil:book ratios varied wildly depending on the source.

Figures released in Tanzania in 1994 suggested that over the previous five years, 94 percent of 17.4 million textbooks printed were delivered to district offices, but that the delivery from district storerooms to schools was uncertain. From statistics of books produced and sent to district levels, book:pupil ratios appeared to be in the region of 1:3 or 1:4.

A trial survey in 1994 on classroom usage of books in Tanzania concluded that book:pupil ratios were somewhat closer to 1:9 and there were extreme variations between schools and districts. A considerable number of books did not reach pupils. They either did not reach the school at all or were being held in school storerooms due to "uncertainty over future supply." An unknown proportion of books were already being purchased by parents, outside of the state system. In other words, parents were beginning to buy free state-produced textbooks from somewhere.

Less well documented is the extent of the industry's dependence on donor support. In the event of donor withdrawal, state systems in most instances would have collapsed. They were not sustainable without support. This triggered serious questioning of prospects for the long-term textbook supply.

Decision making has been a drawn out process, finally embarked on when a government was made to appreciate the extent of the crisis, acutely reflected in falling educational performance.

The Current Situation: Some Major Themes

While the transition to commercialization is in motion in Tanzania, Zambia, Mozambique, and Ethiopia, there appears to be lack of clarity in roles, time frames and operational details of future phases. Nobody knows exactly what their part will be in the machinery of textbook provision, including the consumer.

Without a definitive five-to-ten-year plan, the transition cannot be considered irreversible and yet it is clear donors will not support any reversal. The major element in textbook provision is planning. Any publishing operation relies on thorough planning because publishing itself is a process concerned with management of diverse resources—from authorship to financing, production, and distribution. One textbook may take two to three years to just develop, let alone a publishing program or distribution arrangement. The lack of definitive plans are perhaps understandable. The commercial system, itself underdeveloped and new to everybody involved, needs time to orient itself. Nevertheless, one senses confusion arising from the multiplicity of donors involved, advocating different priorities, subsidizing (and stressing) part but not all of the textbook system.

There is little apparent difference in overall objectives between donors. However, opinions vary considerably over some critical issues. Some donors tend to see indigenous publishing in a prominent role, while for others (including the World Bank) this is not a central issue. There are differences in approach to time frames. The Scandinavians seem committed to the phased and careful expansion of privatization while other donors prefer the fast-track approach. A prominent World

Bank official called for the immediate privatization of textbooks in Tanzania on the grounds that it could not possibly be worse. He maintained that in a sample survey of households, 59 percent expressed discontent with availability of textbooks and that in his view parents could be relied on to pay for textbooks. He suggested that state assets in publishing be auctioned. The basic difference may be summed up as one approach that sees financing the market and freeing production quickly as imperative and another that sees the phased creation of capacity over a longer time frame as critical. The differences in donor approaches have contributed to the problem. In fact, the lack of clear decisions and leadership from these governments, especially in regard to a time frame for the transition, has contributed significantly to the confusion.

It is in the nature of books and education that many government departments and officials are involved in textbook provision. Only a few have professional publishing expertise and those that do have learned their trade under state monopoly. They also have different perspectives and interests in the outcome.

Moreover, the level of sycophancy in many African governments means that many decisions are referred to higher authority. Reaching decisions for this complex process requires careful preparation and has been a persistent problem. Among other effects, this has given external consultants tremendous influence. They enter this milieu as independent and impartial experts, able to prescribe solutions. In itself, this is not a bad thing, if it helps the process along. The problem is that it is a form of dependency. It does not develop the capacity of African governments to take informed and expert decisions in relationship to book provision. It is expensive and impractical to rely completely on external technical input over a transition which will take perhaps eight years. Good technical knowledge is needed locally.

Governments have no experience in operating within a system of private-sector textbook provision. They are understandably cautious or even fearful. Officials and departments used to the state-monopoly approach in many cases hardly know where to begin, and many key decisions are needed rapidly. This is aptly seen in textbook approval systems, where a confusing array of possible approval systems present themselves. Which is the best? How fast can new systems be put into place?

In summary governments, under considerable pressure to effect the transition are unclear about exactly how to proceed. Clear decisions for the medium term (five years) are needed quickly in order for publishers and everyone else involved to begin planning, preparing, and financing. They have not been made. Such decisiveness is hampered by the ministries implementing (rather than managing) the process and having to make too many decisions against a backdrop of inexperience in private-sector textbook provision.

The Indigenous Commercial Sector: The Driving Force

The most worrying element however, is the apparent failure to recognize that the commercial sector must provide the impetus for change and demonstrate the technical proficiency required for textbook provision. The transition will occur successfully only to the extent and at the pace that the commercial sector can replace state textbook provision. An accelerated process is realistic only if the commercial sector is capable of meeting this challenge.

The tendency of ministries of education to retain decision-making authority, with the most important decisions having then to be cleared at a higher level, is worrying. It has the effect of slowing the empowerment of commercial publishing to which many publishing decisions must ultimately be devolved. Rather than being recognized as a full partner in the transition process with the education ministries and donors, the indigenous commercial sector is still a somewhat subdued element.

The problems posed by an infant industry, even one with highly experienced individuals are real and cannot be underestimated, especially as regards financing and infrastructure. If indigenous commercial publishers and booksellers are unprepared for the challenge, the multinationals are not. In an accelerated liberalization, where emerging local publishers and booksellers face financing problems and shortcomings in technical expertise, foreign publishers stand to capture a considerable market share. Ultimately, it will be simply a matter of who is able to develop, publish, and place the manuscripts on the market more quickly. This places the indigenous commercial sector, once again, on the periphery with the exception of the privatized former state monopoly. It is unlikely that sufficient financial resources exist in the emerging local private sector to bear the risks involved with unrestricted competition.

Government's Role: To Implement or Manage
Ministries of education, concerned that an overly abrupt transition will seriously disrupt textbook provision, still perceive their function as one of implementing the transition, rather than "managing" it by delegating state-, private-, and NGO-sector resources to achieve the required results.

Serious flaws are found in this approach. The transition to commercialization is exceptionally difficult. Above all it requires that decision making has to be increasingly decentralized. The decision to publish any book, for instance, ideally must be at the risk of the publisher for the ethos of commercialization to mature. It should be a decision based on assumptions about the market, the product, the competition, financing, and returns. It cannot be effectively made in the "command" style of administration. The strategic problem here is that commercialization of the existing state monopoly does not automatically mean commercialization of the system, which requires competition. How does one break up the monopoly (which provides the books) and introduce the necessary "level playing field" in a situation where books are needed now and not in two or three years?

In Tanzania, the vehicle has been the Swedish International Development Authority-sponsored Pilot Project for Publishing (PPP), which has put selected textbooks out to tender to emerging commercial publishers. It has been an innovative approach. In Mozambique, the Instituto nacionale do livro is actively trying to promote small private publishers, while the former state textbook publisher, Editora escolar, is being privatized. The role of private booksellers in school supplies has been recognized for some years and a commercial "book chain" is emerging. In Ghana, the state has launched a system of copublishing between state and private publishers. In Zambia the newly launched national book policy provides the beginnings of long-term policy.

The PPP in Tanzania, which is a commendable first stage, assumes a degree of centralization and control by the education officials and a gradual withdrawal by the state. It is precisely this withdrawal by the state that is problematic. The state retains a monopoly on all approved core manuscripts and works with specific textbook authors. Commercial publishers only enter the system through a strict but laborious tender procedure. The Ministry of Education retains absolute control of the market by making purchasing decisions centrally. Distribution remains centralized, effectively excluding the booksellers. In this mode of state control there is not enough room for the type of creative entrepreneurship demanded by publishing. Too much centralized planning in implementation exacerbates a bottleneck of decisions in an already overstrained system.

The capacity of the indigenous commercial sector will determine the outcome of privatization. A fundamental weakness is failure to understand why empowerment of this sector is so urgent, why too much central decision making slows the process, and how the problems of an infant industry should be addressed.

Competition

If genuine competition is not achieved, the commercial system will suffer many of the short-comings of the previous state monopoly. Growth, diversity of output, and a long-term commitment to issues such as national culture and language are not possible when one or two multinationals dominate the market.

Publishing in Zimbabwe provides ample evidence of success in this regard. To an overwhelming extent, creative writing, general books, children's books, national-language books, and for that matter book awards are the preserve of the small, struggling indigenous publishers, not the dominant textbook publishers, most of whom are subsidiaries or associates of Longmans and Macmillans.

Competition is only plausible when two conditions are met. First, when some emerging indigenous commercial publishers significantly reduce the financial and technical gap with their vastly bigger state and multinational competitors; and second, when approvals for multiple textbook are in place. It is difficult to comprehend the hesitancy of education officials on the second point. Surely a system where authors and their publishers have to compete openly results in better books and more innovation than a system where only a single author and book is allowed. Moreover, the latter is open to some level of malpractice. It centralizes a critical decision and relies entirely on the integrity and competence of everyone involved. It is not self-regulating.

The Purchasing System

The purchasing system devised will "drive" the new system under privatization. Assuming some form of per capita funding for textbook provision, the critical decision is precisely where and how the purchasing decisions take place. Centralized purchasing, still the case in

Zambia, Tanzania, Ethiopia, and Ghana, reinforces the accumulated habits of the old system. Will schools have a choice of textbook for a subject, which implies competition? Or will purchasing simply mean schools will decide how many copies of the approved textbook they will buy? As a general principle, the further away the purchasing decision is from the actual user of the material, the less efficient the use of the funds.

Devolved purchasing on the other hand brings new problems, and transparency in this regard is essential. Decentralized purchasing can mean decentralized malpractice and problems of incompetence. There is an urgent need to train schools and education officers in the basic methods of purchasing, both on the administrative side and on textbook selection. The way these questions are approached will largely determine the future viability of local publishing and book provision.

Distribution

The number of volumes required for primary school core texts makes centralized supply viable, perhaps even desirable for a limited period. But as soon as one looks further, the distribution capacity of the book trade becomes critical. Upper secondary, tertiary, and professional schools require a greater number of titles and the market is spread more widely and in small pockets.

While it is possible to distribute primary and some secondary core texts through centralized channels, it is impossible with most other types of books. These require many points of sale and channels of access to reach their intended user. Without a healthy book trade infrastructure, potential buyers are without access. Lack of marketing and distribution, through bookshops, seriously inhibits all types of publishing, except large volume primary and secondary texts. This results in viability problems throughout the publishing system. Publishing needs backlists and diversity to strengthen their economic base. Backlists need consumers and many bookshops.

For various reasons countries moving away from state monopoly publishing are still discouraging the development of a book trade. Bookshops are still seen as unnecessary "middle-men", making books more expensive by taking a margin for themselves.

Centralized approaches to distribution appear attractive because through cutting out the retailer, creating a single distribution system, and concentrating supply lines, prices are lower. However, the cost to the book industry and book provision is great.

Bookshops, denied access to 85 percent or more of the market, become commercially untenable, cannot develop, close down, and overall access to books is greatly reduced. General and specialized publishers and lists are retarded. Quality declines with a lack of competition. This is how book industries lapse into a downward spiral of crisis management.

In the long term one must look toward significantly more effective distribution systems than those provided by state monopolies. One cannot promote commercial publishing unless people have access to books, and booksellers have access to the textbook market. It is unlikely that bookshops will develop quickly. It takes a considerable period to develop book trade skills. These are often learned on the job. Both donors and governments need to change their attitudes toward distribution and recognize the function of the bookseller in a commercial book industry. If there are no bookshops, the trade in general books collapses, readership suffers, book "awareness" and book "culture" are undermined, and all of this impacts educational development.

Economies of Scale, Intra-African Trade, Regional Collaboration

If privatization is ultimately to achieve an independent, self-sustaining commercial book sector, rather than simply respond to crisis, it is impossible to avoid issues determined by economies of scale.

As an idea of what this means, two of Africa's more successful book industries combined, Kenya and Zimbabwe, represent a market of perhaps 5 percent of a small European country (such as Norway, Denmark, or the Netherlands) with an unique language and about one-ninth the population of the African nations. From a U.S. dollar per capita angle, Norway's book industry is about 150 times bigger than Zimbabwe's. This monetary comparison does not reflect volume or scope, since African books are about one-fifth the price of Norway's, but the comparison makes the point.

Publishers and book chain systems cannot function if the market they are working in is too small to support some economies of scale. This is particularly acute outside the primary and junior secondary textbook markets. Trapped in small domestic markets African publishers face an overwhelming constraint. In the long term, privatization must be accompanied by government efforts to promote intra-African trade in books, and regional collaboration. African publishers need access to bigger markets to fuel growth.

It is striking that regional approaches to book provision issues are so rarely mentioned. Solutions to certain problems can hardly be addressed unless a regional strategy is devised. Training and printing are examples. Publishing is such a broad activity that no African country will develop the full range of training required. Few countries in Africa will develop the scope of printing needed to service all publishing needs. Printing technology is developing rapidly and the costs of retooling with new technologies are beyond the means of many countries. Where solutions to pressing book problems are elusive at the national level, regional approaches should be explored.

Intra-African trade in books and printing presents considerable potential as a catalyst for improvement in book provision in many countries. In technical and scientific subjects, in some tertiary areas (e.g., teacher training), and often in literature, the curricula or examination demands between several countries are so close as to be nearly identical. This is evidenced partly by the fact that multinational publishers have been able to slightly revise the same text all over Africa to comply with local curricula. Universities, teacher colleges, technical colleges, and other institutions throughout Africa are in many cases using an identical imported text.

The biggest obstacle to intra-African trade is ineffective information and marketing. To add to national bias, tariff barriers, lack of interest by development agencies, misunderstandings from governments, difficulties involved in starting, plus the practical problems of shipping, payments, and foreign currency have all served to inhibit intra-African book trade. It needs help.

The Goal: Getting the Book Chain Functioning

Privatization is merely a step—one of a series of measures aimed at creating a functioning, sustainable book chain. Book provision systems are, in reality, a complex set of linkages, a system of many components, evolved over a long period. This book chain is fragile even in the more robust African book industries. Policy priority must be to get the whole book chain system functioning at its most basic level with all of its components. This is the point from which book development starts in any meaningful way. Producing books and sending them out to schools is not book development until it takes place within a self-sustaining system of book provision. Because this fundamental issue is poorly understood by many civil servants and development professionals, whose background is not in books, lessons are not learned. That books are the basic tool of education in undeniable, but that does not imply that educational experts are therefore the best people to manage book production and supply, or indeed that pedagogical (e.g., curricula) considerations provide the sole rationale in book supply. Book industries operate according to criteria determined by many factors outside the educational system. While educational considerations determine content and use, provision is essentially an industrial issue. Yet, this is precisely what educators forget when they enter into authorship, publishing, production, pricing, and supply and erect monopolistic barriers to exclude all others.

Much of the pain in the emergence of the book chain is still caused by short-term, inappropriate state and donor-influenced policy decisions. Curriculum developers and teachers are still writing books that should be written by a growing pool of semiprofessional writers and editing books that should be edited by publishers. Educational officials are still assuming the role of book distributor and bookseller, another technically demanding occupation, and attempting to manage book distribution systems. In their attempts to assume these roles, government is distorting and retarding the normal emergence of the book chain.

Slowly emerging commercial book industries need financing, incentives, institutional support, and training. They need to operate in an environment relatively and increasingly free of state control, but in the "national interest." They need governments that understand how policy decisions affect the book industry, and how to coordinate these decisions with a long-term strategy to establish an indigenous book industry. Ad hoc decisions, hostility, and neglect will produce erratic performance and the need for constant and unsustainable donor support. While the macroeconomic environment has not helped, neither is it the principle reason why indigenous book industries in many African countries have failed to take root. A start has been made in the decision to privatize state monopolies, but it is only a start.

Unless dire circumstances dictate otherwise, governments should concentrate on achieving basic administrative goals to ensure optimum book use. These include storage, use, and conservation of books in the school system; development of libraries; basic administrative systems to purchase and deliver books to schools; adequate per capita financing of the book costs of the educational system; overseeing book content and quality control; and setting curricula, examinations, and standards. Otherwise the role of government is to ensure appropriate policy for the commercial viability of the book chain to provide the necessary books. This remains a goal, not a reality, but one that should be shared by all. It is a vital component of the book chain and the balance of responsibilities that promotes healthy book provision.

There is no fundamental conflict between the state and private publishing. Each has their role, their responsibility, and the need for close cooperation is essential. However, the economics of publishing industries have been misunderstood and there is a critical need for policymakers and donors to listen to publishing professionals.

This "book chain" view must be extended to professional book institutions and NGOs. Every publishing system needs them and they are in evidence in every successful book industry in the world. Their importance is underestimated in Africa. Indigenous NGOs involved in book development are often more effective than foreign NGOs because they are more responsive to local priorities and sensitive to a changing situation. They are invariably more effective than governments because their objectives are better defined; they specialize in an area of development and are less bureaucratic.

More importantly, local NGOs act as agents of change, defining the needs clearly and introducing new approaches to old problems and changing conditions. They include professional associations and book councils, and their output will include the basic "tools" of book development—statistics and national bibliographies, which have not existed in much of Africa.

A brief, final note is the absolute necessity for a long-term national book policy. It is sometimes said that many successful book industries do not have a "book policy." This is simply not true. It may not be written down in so many words in a document, but policy formulation exists. The main considerations in national book policy are not its content as such, which must change with circumstance, but that all the players—all government departments concerned, the development sector, and the private sector—are involved in and committed to its design; that it is conceived as a continuous, evolving, and flexible process to be modified and improved; and lastly, that it must be implemented, mistakes and all, with government backing.

The effect of book policies in countries such as India, Colombia, and Greece—all somewhat closer to African reality than Western Europe—deserve study to appreciate how significantly book policy, and in some cases legislation, can improve book provision.

3

The Transition to Privatization in Publishing: Ghana's Experience

RICHARD A. B. CRABBE

To speak of privatization in Ghana today evokes memories of how publishing started. The history of publishing is closely linked with the early Christian missionary work. As early as 1870, the Basel Mission opened a book depot in the then Gold Coast (Osei, 1994). From then until the second half of the twentieth century, publishing was in private hands. Since the Church led the way in education and literacy work, it controlled much of the publishing done in the country. Local publishing started with the production of Bibles, hymnbooks, and liturgical material. In 1900 only a few Africans (Ghanaians) could read. By 1945, literacy had increased considerably (Hildebrandt, 1991).

The earliest government intervention came in 1951, when the government set up the Vernacular Literature Bureau, now the Bureau of Ghana Languages, to publish primers and postliteracy materials in selected Ghanaian languages to support the Mass Education Program. The government also set up the Ghana Universities Press in 1962 to "undertake scholarly publishing of the findings of the universities" (Osei, 1994).

After independence in 1957, the government's interventions gradually increased. The accelerated Development Plan of 1961, the Free Textbooks Scheme of 1963, and the Investment Decree of 1976 firmly established the state as the leading publisher in Ghana (Nimako, 1991). Between 1961 and 1974, textbooks for primary schools were written by Ghanaians and published by British multinational publishing houses. After 1974, the Ministry of Education decided to publish its own materials (Djoleto, 1989). In Nimako's words:

> The Ministry of Education has organized writing workshops and has commissioned panels of subject experts to write textbooks for Primary, Junior Second-

ary and Senior Secondary Schools. It has bought print for the production of the books in the country and outside it. (Nimako, 1991).

From conception stage through writing, production, distribution and usage, the government came to control practically all aspects of educational publishing in the country.

The Free Textbooks Scheme

As detailed above this scheme greatly weakened the indigenous publishing industry. In his draft "Proposals for the Formulation of New Book Policy for the Ghana Education Sector," Djoleto (1989) points out that

> ... the most destructive, though unwritten, rule in practice, that goes with the Free Textbooks Scheme is this: If the state provides no books, pupils shall buy no books to use in school and should use no books whatever at school. No matter whether suitable alternative or even MOE (Ministry of Education) approved private Ghana book industry sector books are available for pupils to buy and use in class even as a stop-gap, pupils must use no books so long as FTS (Free Textbooks Scheme) itself has not supplied schools any.

It is more depressing to read from Djoleto that the result has been that

> most children who have been or are still in the public (state-run school) system have no reading habit and in several distressing cases cannot read at all. . . . They do not learn the importance of book buying throughout life. . . . In these circumstances children have no way of developing library culture for themselves.

These are strong words coming from the (then) textbooks consultant for Ghana's Ministry of Education. As Nimako succinctly put it: "By capturing educational publishing at its most profitable level, the state (has) left very little for private indigenous houses to hang on to (Nimako, 1991)."

Ghanaian publishers could hardly penetrate the market at the preuniversity level with the few textbooks and supplementary readers they published. Ironically, during this same period, the government was contracting foreign (multinational) companies to publish for the educational market, virtually shutting out local publishers and further deepening the difficulties indigenous publishing houses had to face.

In 1984, the government entered into an agreement with five local publishers to copublish certain textbooks for primary schools. The Co-publishing Project, as the agreement was called, was to team up "state, parastatal and the private sector of the Ghana national book industry, pooling their resources to publish core textbooks for formal education in Ghana" (Djoleto, 1989). This agreement also permitted the publishers to produce extra print runs of the textbooks for sale to the public. At its introduction, Djoleto notes, the Co-publishing Project was a "unique, first-of-its-kind effort in all Africa," designed to encourage private participation in the textbook market.

It is noteworthy that although the agreement was signed in 1984, implementation began in 1990—six years later! Taken in perspective, this move by government had little positive impact on the Ghanaian publishing industry as a whole. The agreement covered only selected textbooks—thirty titles, for primary schools. Thus, the majority of textbooks for the junior secondary and senior secondary levels remained unavailable to students on the open market.

By 1991, not more than fourteen registered publishers were active. A new aspect of publishing, appropriately called "self-publishing," had emerged and had begun to compete with the already weakened publishing companies. Many manuscripts were produced in mimeographed (sometimes barely legible) print on duplicating machines, by the writers, often teachers, and well-known examiners for the respective subject areas. Students happily purchased these texts, as they found the material vital to their chances of being successful in examinations, more so as it was their teachers who sold them.

Writers

The availability of competent writers has not been a problem. From the period before independence from British colonial rule until now, local writers have held their own in Africa and the rest of the world. Ghanaian writers like Asare Konadu, Atukwei Okai, Amu Djoleto, Efua T. Sutherland, Ama Atta Aidoo, Ayikwei Armah, Meshack Asare, and Austin Amissah received international recognition for their works.

Atukwei Okai became founding secretary-general of the Pan-African Writers Association, while Meshack Asare and Austin Amissah both won the Noma Award for Publishing, Africa's most prestigious publishing prize. The proliferation of self-published, duplicated material also highlighted the abundance of unpublished writers for the educational market.

Financing and Profitability

This has been a major problem for publishers over the years. Given the history and state of affairs described above, it has been virtually impossible for publishers to obtain loans from their bankers. As a result, undercapitalization has dogged the industry. This has resulted in low print runs throughout the book industry. On the average, publishers print fewer than 3,000 copies of a book. Even then, an unsuccessful book could push the publisher dangerously close to bankruptcy.

In 1995, one bank decided to offer loans to publishers. It was the first bank to make book publishing part of its lending portfolio. To date, however, the opportunity has not been snapped up due to the high prevailing interest rate, 45 percent minimum. It must be pointed out that the high interest rate is a reflection of the economic climate in the country, and not something directed specifically at the publishing sector.

So, how have publishers survived? Publishers have shown creativity and resilience by, generating capital for themselves through selling paper, publishing for the growing children's market, and making credit deals with printers. Sometimes this means that the printer releases limited quantities to the publisher as payment is effected. Obviously this affects marketing and sales plans as well as the volume of print runs.

Profitability is influenced by three major factors, as identified by Alec Gilmore (Gilmore, 1996):

1. Size of Market: as already stated, educational publishing constitutes the largest percentage and the most profitable portion of publishing in the country and the government continues to hold a virtual monopoly on this.

2. Purchasing Power: conventional thinking is that people in rural areas (the majority of the population) will not be able to afford books. Information gathered by the Ghana Book Publishers Association (GBPA) from its district book fairs (held 1992–1995 with financial support from the Canadian Organization

for Development through Education/CODE), shows that this may only be true for certain books and for certain areas. Many people, especially children, have willingly bought books, ranging from textbooks to general readers. Children have even used their lunch money to buy books for themselves. Over a three-day period, total sales during the book fairs have ranged from a low of 1.5 million cedis to 22 million cedis (1,400 cedis = U.S. $1.00) for an average of twelve publishers per fair.

3. Unrealistic Expectations: publishers have erroneously expected that people will buy anything. Times have changed and we now have a discriminating public, looking for quality (Nimako and Boye, 1996).

Does profitability matter? Gilmore (1996) argues that:
> If profitability is such a problem to achieve, why worry about it? Why not just accept that donor aid will be necessary until some time in the distant future, when the general economy of less-developed countries would reach a point where self-sufficiency could become a practical possibility?

But it would be unwise to use donor aid without developing the necessary infrastructure that would enable a country to move toward the self-sufficiency that Gilmore writes about. Without incorporating the need to make money into the development of the industry, the foundation that is laid is likely to encourage stagnation or even collapse.

He further states:
> Most aid and development agencies work on the principle of creating and establishing local activities. Publishing, if it is to be taken seriously as a development effort, must work on the same basis.

Probably the strongest point Gilmore makes is the following:
> Self-respect requires that indigenous publishing attains independence from the policies and funds of Western donors. It is important that they escape from this feeling of dependency and inferiority.

Trends Since 1992

Since 1992, the climate has begun to change. But the winds of change have been blowing slowly, and painfully so. It is remarkable that this period also signifies the democratic era ushered in by the 4th Republic. In reviewing this period, one needs to consider the issues of policy formulation, publishing capacity (personnel, printing facilities, distribution) and reading habits, as well as the possible effects these issues would have on the quality of education, the development of the private book publishing industry, and the general economy of the country. Probably the most important aspects to consider would be the impact of a policy privatizing the industry and the attitudes of officials toward practitioners in the Ghana book industry.

No official policy exists. In a very real sense, the book publishing industry has never officially been controlled by the government. But, as described above, educational publishing, which has represented the bulk of the market since the attainment of independence from colonial rule, has been monopolized by the government. Thus in the general climate of openness that has prevailed in the country since the beginning of the 4th Republic in January 1993, publishers have been lobbying officials of the Ministry of Education for more access to the textbook market and better recognition, acceptance and promotion of their books.

The first step toward effective lobbying was to create a strong, respected voice. Toward this goal the GBPA was revived in 1992 by former members and now comprises fifty-two bona fide publishers, up from fourteen at the end of 1991. This has been achieved with the financial support of CODE, which has enabled the GBPA to open and operate a secretariat. The next step was to organize seminars and workshops to improve the quality of personnel in the book industry.

Members of the association met with the minister of education, his two deputies, and top officials in September 1993. It was the first time in the history of publishing in Ghana that the sector minister had held such a meeting with publishers to discuss matters affecting the book industry. At the meeting, publishers asked for access to the syllabi used throughout the school system, from primary to senior secondary level, a more open system of recommending supplementary readers to schools, provision of funding to enable the Ghana Library Board to purchase books on a regular basis, a review of the prevailing practice of using only one textbook per subject in schools, and the setting aside of a percentage of all book projects (under the World Bank's International Competitive Bidding Scheme) for local publishers in furtherance of building capacity in the Ghanaian book industry.

Although a follow-up meeting promised by the minister has not materialized, publishers, through the GBPA, now have more access to top officials (even to get information) at the ministry than in the past. The syllabi used in the educational system were virtually guarded like "official secrets" before this meeting, but are now available to publishers.

Prior to the September meeting, entrepreneurs in the book industry had asked the Ministry of Education to demonopolize its hold on the publishing of textbooks needed by the country's educational system (Tamakloe,1993).

It is interesting that participants at the seminar, which was attended by officials of publishing houses in both private and public sectors, pointed out that the practice by which local publishers were sidelined when it came to contracting for the publication of textbooks in the country was disheartening. They contended that "unless publishing was accorded its proper role and the Ministry ceased to compete with the private publishing sector . . . the local (publishing) sector would not grow." Further, participants called on the ministry to involve them in formulating its publishing policies and curriculum development to enable private publishers to keep abreast of its demands.

Policy Formulation

In the privatized economy that the government has committed to, book production ought to be in the hands of private entrepreneurs. But what is more serious is that no national book policy exists. Djoleto presented his proposals in 1989, but the document, which includes an excellent analysis of book procurement procedures used by the Ministry of Education since the early 1960s, has yet to receive the attention it deserves. If such a policy exists, it does so only on paper or is known only to certain officials of the Ministry of Education. Nothing has been made public.

This point needs to be addressed if the book industry is to become truly privatized. Before a national book policy is announced, all aspects should be clearly articulated and discussed openly to take into account the views of all participants in the book industry. In Djoleto's proposals, he targeted 1995 as the year by which this cooperation for mutual benefit would have been firmly and fully established. As of 1996, the winds of change had yet to reach this area of policy formulation.

When publishers ask for involvement in formulating policy, it is because so much of it will ultimately affect the bulk of their industry. (What books will be required and in what quantities? When, where, and how should such books be produced? Will those books be used primarily in libraries or in schools?)

It seems also that there is a basic misconception at various levels of decision making in government circles as to who a publisher is. Quite often, publishers are confused with printers. As a result, publishers are regarded as those whose services will only be required when the ministry has produced texts for publication. That mindset has to change as a basic step toward fully privatizing the industry.

At the time of writing, a draft for the government's proposed Free and Compulsory Universal Basic Education program has been prepared. In the process, publishers were again sidelined. The existence of such a document only came to the attention of the GBPA council by accident. Ghana cannot achieve the goal of a sustainable literary environment if the government continues to ignore publishers, who are largely responsible for the availability of books on the market and who coordinate the activities of writers, editors, designers, illustrators, printers, and booksellers to ensure that books get into the hands of readers.

Obviously, then, an information gap exists between the ministry, on the one hand, and the practitioners within the book industry (especially publishers) on the other. It is critical to the development and growth of a viable book publishing industry in Ghana that the role of private, indigenous publishers receive full recognition "as indispensable to sound education in Ghana and not just encouraged but actively patronized by the government to that end" (Djoleto, 1989).

It is understandable if, in the area of textbooks, the Ministry of Education retains overall responsibility for the curriculum. But it would certainly help both the ministry and book publishers if the latter were involved in various aspects of policy formulation. Publishers are concerned that even now, the ministry prescribes only one textbook per subject studied in schools. Why not have a list of recommended textbooks for each subject? This would create more competition among publishers, and improve the quality of production and marketing of what is available. This used to be the case in the early 1960s. Parents could then buy according to what book(s) the teacher would select for a particular subject.

Publishing Capacity
Government officials have often questioned the ability of local publishers to satisfy the demands of the educational market. It is important, therefore to examine carefully some of the key elements of publishing capacity and to determine whether Ghanaian publishers can

effectively meet the demands of this undertaking.

As already stated, the number of active publishers in Ghana has grown from 14 in 1991 to 52 today. These range from small publishers (minimum of two books per year) to larger ones producing at least 20 titles each year. Combined, these publishers produce up to 300 titles per annum. Several of these titles have already been assessed and approved by the Ministry of Education as suitable for classroom use. Publishers assert that if five publishers have successfully handled the Co-publishing Agreement involving 30 books for primary schools, which usually need larger print runs than do the secondary schools levels, there is every reason that the GBPA should feel confident that its fifty-two members can effectively produce all 104 of the titles listed as required school textbooks for the open market. Since 1988, the GBPA has been running seminars and workshops aimed at developing and improving staff skills, as well as improving the quality of books produced in the country. This has benefited more than 200 staff at all levels of operation, from front office staff to senior management. Any person looking over the quality of books produced by Ghanaian publishers during the period from 1988 to the present will definitely see marked improvement in the editorial and production quality of the books.

Graduates of the Book Industry Degree Programme of the University of Science and Technology (UST), Kumasi, have further upgraded the talent available to publishers today. In 1995, the program was accorded full departmental status by the UST.

Before 1990 there was only one printer who could handle the large print runs needed by schools. Today, there are at least five such printing presses, all well-equipped with the latest technology. These would still be inadequate for the country's needs, but nothing stops a publisher from outsourcing printing in the Far East or other economically attractive places. After all, publishers argue, those multinationals which have published for Ghana's educational system have not necessarily printed all of what was required locally.

As part of its program of privatizing Ghana's economy, the government has decided to divest part of its ownership in the Ghana Publishing Corporation (Daily Graphic, 1996). Two divisions, the Tamale Press in the northern region of Ghana and the Takoradi Press in the western region, are for sale. Essentially, these are printing houses. The Publishing Division and the Tema Press have not been advertised as being "for sale," but there are rumors that they may also be sold.

In time, Ghana's printing industry will grow. As of now, the bulk of its output is not book production. It must be pointed out that unless the government creates the opportunity for growth, local printers will continue to cater mainly to areas other than the book industry.

Given the opportunity, Ghanaian publishers can also develop the capacity to compete effectively with their international counterparts who win tenders through competitive bidding for book publishing projects in Ghana financed by World Bank loans. Unless indigenous publishers develop the capacity to compete, successive generations of Ghanaians will end up repaying loans that would not have built up the local publishing industry. In fact, the loans will have paid to improve publishing industries in countries where the industry is already well established.

Distribution and Sales

The weakness inherent in the existing distribution system through private means has already been mentioned. This by no means indicates that the sector cannot grow. In fact, one should expect that if private publishing gains more access to the large educational market, bookshops, and other distribution outlets, it will grow. Healthy competition has a way of generating quality service to the benefit of the customer. While the ministry may continue to purchase books according to its specific needs, marketing, and distribution of the books throughout the country really should be in the hands of publishers and booksellers.

Before 1963, book procurement was a private affair (Djoleto, 1989). The school culture itself during that time encouraged the development of the book buying and reading habit for life. Djoleto further states that:

> as private sector or open market organized distribution or sale to schools, the book depots or bookshops became the bedrock of the entire book trade of the country, including religious and general books.

The main setback has been that the bookshops did not cover the entire country; most were based in the major cities in the southern part of Ghana. On the parastatal side, the Ghana Publishing Corporation (GPC) in its best years had five branches in Accra (the capital) alone and nineteen scattered throughout the rest of the country. In the private sector, the bookseller with the widest network has been the Methodist Book Depot, which used to have twelve to fifteen bookshops and distribution points throughout the country.

Today, not more than five of the Depot's bookshops remain actively involved in stocking all kinds of books. Only one bookseller, Challenge Enterprises, specializing in Christian books, and the Bible Society, with its Bibles and New Reader portions, make an effort to cover the whole country. Even then, they rely heavily on colporteurs to distribute supplies to remote areas on a regular basis.

Many more bookshops are needed, with real potential for at least 80 to 90 in district capitals (Ghana has 110 districts) around the country. This is a challenge for booksellers and a fertile avenue for investment. But booksellers say they would first have to be sure they would receive the books to sell, before opening outlets in various parts of the country. The economic viability of such an enterprise is closely linked with demand for and availability of the books. It needs to be recognized that booksellers are in business to make money and will pursue any good opportunities that come their way.

To some extent, then, the ministry is right in purchasing quantities of textbooks for distribution to schools outside the major cities. But despite building a nationwide distribution network, the Ministry of Education is itself still unable to provide textbooks for every pupil. In fact, economic realities show that it cannot and will never be able to provide books to meet the needs of every pupil, even in the primary schools.

Publishing for the Open Market

As already stated, the Co-publishing Agreement permitted the publishers involved to reprint quantities of those titles for sale to the general public. This has proved largely successful as an experiment in privatizing textbook publishing. In the wake of this success, however, other problems have surfaced. First, it has been established that copies produced for the government and not for sale have found their way onto the market. Some of these have actually been stolen from government supplies. The publishers have made suggestions for redesigning the covers to show more clearly what is for public sale. Second, in some instances clear cases of piracy by printers or individuals exploiting the high demand for the books have been uncovered. In one case, a salesperson actually offered a publisher some of the publisher's own titles at a price much lower than the market price.

The situation proved to be even worse than it first appeared when police were called in to investigate the matter and found that the printer responsible had large stocks of titles licensed to other publishers as well.

The GBPA is working with the Copyright Administrator and the Copyright Society of Ghana (COSGA) to educate the public and top government officials about the effects of book piracy on the industry and on Ghana's international image.

To commemorate UNESCO's first World Book and Copyright Day (April 23, 1996), the above-mentioned organizations teamed up to highlight the growing incidence of piracy and the need to expose and stamp out the practice in order to protect practitioners in the book industry. Existing legislation has to be revised to cover more modern means of reproducing printed matter.

It is clear from monitoring the market that the two problems mentioned (theft of government stocks and piracy) will not go away if demand continues to outstrip supply. In the meantime, demand remains high and textbooks marked "Government Property, Not for Sale" continue to appear on the market.

The GBPA, late in 1994, began negotiating with the Ministry of Education to license Ghanaian publishers to reprint all required textbooks up to senior secondary level. It took nearly eighteen months after the GBPA submitted a draft agreement to the ministry, for approval to come. This is an opportunity for publishers to prove themselves capable of meeting the demands of the textbook market. Alas, the wheels of officialdom turn ever so slowly.

If the private sector reprints the textbooks, the government would not have to provide subsidy. Some officials have voiced concern about keeping costs low. In fact, Djoleto (1989) suggested that "the Ministry of Education should have a determining say in the fixing of prices of core textbooks sold on the open market to forestall irresponsible speculation." He stated that there should be an agreed upon sales procedure, similar to the Net Book Agreement in the United Kingdom, which would guarantee the same price throughout the country for a particular title. Such a position, despite its advantages, mitigates against the very ethos of privatization, which would be to allow market forces to determine prices. The Net Book Agreement ceased to operate in the United Kingdom in October 1995.

Publishers have concentrated efforts on the key issue that affects the pricing of books—the high cost of producing books locally. This, in turn, is influenced by the tariffs on production inputs. All equipment, paper, inks, films, and plates attract some tariff. Finished books coming into the country enter free from any tariffs. In November 1995, a book of 144 pages printed in Hong Kong and shipped to Ghana was found to cost at least 50 percent less than it would have cost to produce in Ghana without any shipping charges for the same print run..

In February 1996, the GBPA's lobbying efforts succeeded in getting the government to waive the prevailing 15 percent sales tax on all inputs for book publishing imported by its members for their work. An application for exemption from customs duties is currently receiving attention. The GBPA sees the waivers as positive incentives for book production as well as a means of bringing down the prices of books.

Libraries

Libraries play a vital role in inculcating and sustaining the habit of reading. They also create a sales outlet for book publishers. Since the early 1980s the network of libraries operated by the government-run Ghana Library Board (GLB) has suffered from lack of funding for new purchases. Staff have pointed out that local publishers do not produce "library copies," hardcover versions of their titles. Publishers have countered that they would do so if the GLB would guarantee purchases in appreciable quantities as titles are released. That the GLB simply cannot do; it simply does not have the cash. Since 1993, for example, the GLB has not purchased books from publishers in any significant quantities although publishers have dutifully sent samples to the board.

One organization that has filled the gap is the Ghana Book Trust, established with financial support from CODE. The trust has, for the past three years, purchased an average of about 20 million cedis (U.S. $15,000) from members of the GBPA. The program has included fifty to seventy titles written by Ghanaians and published by Ghanaian publishers. The trust has distributed these books to community libraries—libraries set up by towns throughout the country. To compensate for the lack of textbooks in schools, especially in the rural areas, the trust has sometimes purchased some of these for distribution in addition to general reading books. Some school libraries have also benefited in this way.

To develop the reading habit from a very early age, Djoleto (1989) had called for the establishment of libraries in all primary schools, with funds from "Parent-Teacher Associations, public-spirited persons, neighborhoods and communities." He stressed:

> that a library period (not just classroom reading) should not only be built into the timetable of every basic education institution in Ghana but also indeed utilized as such in the school library itself.

Some schools have established libraries, but no figures are available on the number in operation, their stock levels, and their spread throughout the country. It is also difficult to estimate their success, precisely whether these libraries have improved reading habits.

General Publishing

A significant portion of this discussion has covered the publishing of textbooks. This is simply because it forms the greater share of the market, with (subsequent) large print runs and profits. But since textbook publishing has been dominated by the government, publishers have focused on publishing supplementary readers, fiction, and, increasingly, books for children. Most publishers have some children's books as part of their list and see the children's market as an area of potential growth.

With bookshops moving more into stationery over the years, these books have been sold through schools, often directly by the publishers themselves. Some publishers have opened bookshops, with three opening up since 1993. All of these have been in Accra, the capital city. A growing number of publishers are resorting to moving their books around, a kind of "books on wheels" sales force.

The GBPA's district book fairs, three each year since 1993, have promoted the books in seven out of the ten regions of Ghana. Held with financial assistance from CODE, the fairs have targeted children— today's readers being cultivated as tomorrow's buyers. In conjunction with the Children's Literature Foundation and with the support of the Ghana Education Service and the Ghana Book Development Council, GBPA members displaying and selling books have organized "outreach sales"to villages and towns in the rural settings away from district capitals.

In some cases, books sent to these areas have sold out, outstripping what was purchased even in the more affluent district capitals. The eagerness and excitement with which children and their teachers have bought books, sometimes stampeding to get to the book tables, clearly indicate both the interest people have and the extent to which they have been starved of reading material.

The fairs have also highlighted the fact that if privatization is to succeed, publishers would have to promote their books much better than in the past. In one district capital, the paramount chief (traditional head), a well-educated man, remarked: "Are all these books really produced in Ghana? I did not even know we had so many publishers." After touring the stands as part of the official opening ceremony, he returned to his palace and sent his daughter to purchase a large quantity of books to form the nucleus of a library for his people.

Publishing In Ghanaian Languages
During the missionary era of the nineteenth and early twentieth centuries, the bulk of publishing was done in local languages. The Basel Mission, which spawned the Presbyterian Church of Ghana, pioneered writing in the local language, with hymn books and the translation of the Bible in the Akuapem and Ga languages. The Wesleyan Mission, which gave birth to the Methodist Church also produced similar material in Mfantse, and the Bremen Mission did the same in the Ewe language. The Basel missionaries even produced textbooks for subjects like agriculture and arithmetic in the Akuapem language as they built schools.

The colonial period gradually eroded local languages into second-class status. It became a mark of respect if one could speak the King's English (after King George of Britain). Speaking one's own language symbolized backwardness. That was to change after the first self-government took office in 1951 and established the Vernacular Literature Bureau. This metamorphosed into the Bureau of Ghana Languages after independence from colonial rule in 1957.

Apart from the Bureau of Ghana Languages, only three other book publishers produced books in Ghanaian languages before 1992. Even then these publishers did not have more than a combined total of ten titles. One must mention as exceptions the Bible Society and the Ghana Institute of Linguistics, Literacy and Bible Translation (GILLBT), which have published several "New Reader" booklets and portions of the Bible. For more than twenty years, the GILLBT promoted literacy in the lesser-known languages in Ghana creating a growing number of people who can now read and write their own language.

Today, it is official government policy that children in school have to study one local language during nine years of basic education. The Ministry of Education also runs a Non-Formal Education Division (NFED) aimed at promoting literacy primarily among the adult population in the rural areas. The NFED has identified fifteen languages spread around the country for its literacy work.

Naturally, the work of the GILLBT and the NFED has resulted in increasing readership of people literate in the local languages. To meet the needs of the newly literate, the NFED entered into agreement with the GBPA in 1992 to produce various reading materials, including books. Currently twelve publishers are working on 154 book manuscripts covering the fifteen languages in a project worth 640 million cedis (approximately U.S. $460,000). The size of print runs, some as low as 2,000, has meant that the government has had to provide subsidies, 90 percent of production costs in some cases. Publishers will have full responsibility for developing the content of the books, marketing, promotion and sales. The project has been designed so that subsidy levels fall considerably with successive years. Publishers taking part have sometimes complained that since the government controls the funds, officials tend to dictate terms. A joint committee comprised of representatives from the NFED and the GBPA meets when it is necessary to iron out problems and to discuss guidelines. This is a positive development, but, it is a partnership where the government is the funding agency. Ultimately, publishers will have to provide their own capital.

Summary and Recommendations

Across the developing world, Structural Adjustment Programs, put in place by governments acting on the advice of the World Bank and the International Monetary Fund, has begun to create private access to areas that used to be under state control. Ghana's economy is no exception. As Ghana's publishers have struggled to regain what was once their preserve, some issues have surfaced that could form the basis of a checklist for privatizing the book industry.

- The right political climate must exist, guaranteeing the freedom of expression and the freedom to publish. Further, the government must have the political will to turn state publishing enterprises over to private enterprise.
- There should be a clear-cut, well-articulated, open policy for the

process, developed with meaningful input from the industry. In the absence of this, all the players involved—publishers, government officials, writers, booksellers, printers, readers—will suffer considerable frustration.
- All sides must have and demonstrate mutual respect for each other. Government officials must consider publishers as partners, key contributors to the process of sustainable book provision, not simply people out to make money. Without this positive attitude, discussions and negotiations will break down; mistrust will adversely affect relationships.
- It is in the interest of publishers to have a strong, united voice. As far as is possible, they should form an association and empower their leaders to speak on their behalf, "marketing" their industry. The GBPA has been successful in its lobbying efforts because its leaders have had the full backing of the members. It has raised its profile by publicizing its programs and problems in the media and by meeting face-to-face with officials in government and the World Bank on issues as they have arisen.
- Where business details are concerned, each publisher should be free to act independently. Neither the association nor the government should attempt to fix prices of books, for example.
- Publishers need to be creative in the way they tackle the issue of privatization. If the government is unwilling to release its grip on textbook publishing, for example, members of the GBPA need to explore ways of producing them in partnership.
- Quality always speaks for itself. The quality of work produced by publishers in Ghana is one of the strongest statements they can make about their ability to handle a privatized industry.
- The period of transition will vary according to the context. In economies where state control has been the norm for several years, particularly in countries where government has controlled book publishing since independence, transition may take longer. The local private industry may either be starting from scratch or it may have to deal with issues like inflation.
- Book publishing should be recognized as an industry, worthy of support (financially, too) and encouragement by governments. In the drive for export trade, officials in charge of privatizing economies need to realize that books have the potential to generate income for their

countries.
- Everybody stands to win in privatization—writers, editors, publishers, printers, booksellers, teachers, readers, parents, and governments. As such, all sectors need to work together to ensure the success of the process.

Conclusion

Ghana's book industry is once again on the rise. Full privatization has still a long way to go. But given the right nurturing from within the industry and by government, Ghana's book industry has the potential to thrive, expand and achieve excellence. It is remarkable that the industry has boldly set out to carve an international image by hosting its first International Book Fair in Accra in November 1996. Appropriately, the fair aspires to be the publishing marketplace in Africa.

References

Djoleto, S. A. A. 1989. Proposals for the Formulation of a New Book Policy for the Ghana Education Sector.

Gilmore, A. 1996. Publish For Profit. *Interlit* (March): 4–6.

Hildebrandt, J. 1990. *History of the Church in Africa*. Achimota, Ghana: Africa Christian Press.

Nimako, A. 1991. The State of the Book Industry in Ghana—An overview. *Ghana Book World* (5): 1–8.

Nimako A. & Boye, M. 1996. A Critique Of Children's Books Published In Ghana. Paper presented at Seminar on Quality in Children's Literature held in Accra, February, 1996.

Osei, Bonsu 1994. Improving the Book Industry. *Daily Graphic* (Ghana), February 22, 7.

Tamakloe A. 1993. Ministry Urged to De-Monopolise Textbooks. *Ghanaian Times*, July 28.

4
Privatization and the Challenges for Publishing in Ethiopia

ATNAFU WASSIE

No one can doubt the negative effect of the state's dominant role in book development and publishing in Ethiopia in the past. With the growing emphasis on educational reforms, the pressures and responsibilities facing the state are immense. In particular, the development, distribution, and availability of textbooks will require a new approach in view of the socioeconomic, cultural, and political importance of improving education. In addition, school and public libraries will have to be revitalized. According to the new constitution, the Ministry of Education is responsible for the implementation of national education policy. Significant adjustments will be required in the area of textbook policy. The government continues to supervise and control the suitability of program content as well as the availability of books and other related materials. Much will need to be changed. One cannot look at the production of the new educational materials separately from the development needs of the publishing industry as a whole.

The state has also specified a clear policy on privatization, and there is no doubt that initiatives taken so far will encourage growth in the publishing industry.

> Private sector participation shall be promoted in the provision and assistance of the educational service. Different cost-sharing mechanisms shall be studied and introduced....[1]

Much, however, remains to be done. The new privatization agency has to pay special attention to the publishing sector. New incentives will be required in order for publishers and booksellers to initiate or expand activities. The process of the state's disengagement from its long monopoly of textbook publishing, printing, and distribution has not yet been initiated; it should be planned and coordinated on a short- and long-term basis. Strategies must be based on existing circumstances and future goals. This should result in the gradual development of indigenous publishing.

This chapter will focus attention on the publishing industry in

Ethiopia, to recognize the importance of the industry and its unrealized potential. It presents the publishing industry in the context of past developments and current problems. The objective here is to provide information about the Ethiopian case to professionals, government authorities, experts, and members of the development community working at all levels of book development, locally and abroad.

Country, People, and Culture

Ethiopia is an agricultural country; science and modern technology have been integrated to a very limited degree into the economy. With a wealth of natural and human resources, Ethiopia possesses considerable socioeconomic potential. Within the new federal and democratic administrative structures, power has been decentralized at all levels of political administration. In contrast to the recent past, political stability and peace (essential elements for development) have been achieved. Different nations and different nationalities with a rich cultural diversity inhabit the land. The population was estimated to be 56 million in 1995, with an annual growth rate of 3 percent. Half of the population is below fifteen.[2] Though school enrollment has improved in the past few years at all levels, all school-age children still do not attend school. The table below gives a better view of the situation. The decline in enrollment figures after 1987/88 was due to high dropout rates. This is expected to decrease drastically in the coming two decades as a result of the new educational plan.

In 1992/93, there were a total of seventeen technical and vocational schools throughout the country with 2,589 students and 338 teachers. There were twelve institutions of teacher training in 1993/94 with

Table 1
School Statistics, 1967/68–1993/94[3]

Year	Pupils			Teachers			Schools		
	Primary	Junior	Senior	Primary	Junior	Senior	Primary	Junior	Senior
1967/68	451,557	44,777	26,690	9,525	1,694	1,408	1,712	316	84
1977/78	1,143,207	143,880	135,704	28,816	2,347	3,510	4,286	659	147
1987/88	2,884,033	464,016	378,734	58,400	9,283	9,303	8,373	1,064	272
1993/94	2,283,638	357,428	357,194	75,736	10,611	10,987	8,674	1,167	303

5,747 students and 320 teachers. There were about fourteen institutions of higher learning offering undergraduate and postgraduate degrees in various fields including natural science, language studies, social science, business and economics, technology, medical science, pharmacy education, law, veterinary, medicine, library sciences, teachers training, agriculture, forestry, water technology, urban planning, and health science, etc. In 1993/94 the total number of students and teachers in higher education was 15,438 and 2,215, respectively.[4]

Written Culture
Ethiopia is the cradle of one of the oldest civilizations in the world. It has one of the oldest written languages, dating back many centuries. It also has unique natural and socioeconomic conditions. Its cultural and economic activities are the result of the integration of many African and Asian cultures over centuries. The country also integrated Christianity and Islam. Its population is characterized by national and ethnic variations reflecting many common characteristics resulting from a long process of assimilation.

Ethiopia has a long history of writing and literature. The growth and development of culture and the technology of book production was related to the spread of religion within the country. Geez, which started in the fourth century A.D., is one of the oldest alphabets of the world. Historically it can be traced to Axum (northern Ethiopia); it reached its peak between the fourth and seventh centuries. It was the main language of literature in ancient times. The Bible was translated into Geez from Greek between the fourth and seventh centuries. Ornamenting books with elaborate artistic designs was common. Writing, copying, and binding used to be done by the same person who also illustrated books. Materials like vellum, ink, reed, pen, wooden boards, leather, cotton, cloth, silk, gut string, and brocade were used. Manuscripts were written on parchment.[5] Church schools used these manuscripts for teaching, reflecting the tradition in Ethiopian education of written materials and the importance of books, even centuries ago.

New developments in literature began in the thirteenth century A.D., with the replacement of the Geez language by Amharic. This development occurred with the gradual movement of political and cultural life toward the south of the country and away from Axum, the "cradle" of civilization. Amharic became the language of communication, after replacing Geez as the language of the court, but Geez continued to be used as the language of the church. Written works like the "Book of Psalms" and "The Song of Songs" were printed in Geez in Rome and Cologne in the early sixteenth century. A Geez translation of the New Testament was printed in Rome in 1548.[6] Written Amharic evolved from Geez script. Official chronicles were written in Amharic. Missionaries also used it.

Arabic and Islamic literature flourished in Ethiopia. As Islam advanced in northeast Africa, it left its imprint on Ethiopia leaving in its way many stable city-states. Arabic literature grew and developed among the Muslim communities in Ethiopia from the ninth century onwards. Schools for the study of the Koran became important institutions of learning. Ultimately, continuous wars, that originated outside and inside Ethiopia, followed by political, social, and economic degeneration deprived post-Axum Ethiopia of the opportunity for sustainable development. The literary collections deteriorated and the spirit of creativity declined.

The History of Printing and Publishing

The printing of books started in northern Ethiopia (in what is known today as Eritrea) in the town of Massawa (and later, in Keren) in the seventeenth century. Catholic missionaries ran the printing presses. This development moved from north to south. Amharic grammar and other books were printed in 1857, then Geez grammar books in 1872.[7] In 1898 the first printing house was founded in the capital.[8] Following that, books and newspapers by local authors began to be appear. The Ministry of Education assumed responsibility for textbook production. Later, with the emergence of new social and political institutions, private and commercial publishing appeared, including the Oxford Printing Press and the Voice of the Gospel publication services.[9]

A handwritten weekly newspaper was introduced at the end of the nineteenth century marking the foundation of mass media. With the establishment of printing presses, newspapers and magazines began to appear in French and Amharic.[10] Newspapers and magazines were printed in Tigrai and English as well. The publications were low in quality and had limited circulation. A small book production center for primary education was established in 1957, marking the beginning of textbook production under the authority of the Ministry of Education. By 1960, 243 titles of books and pamphlets for school purposes were designated for publication in "experimental" editions; 21 of them were imported titles.[11]

The period from 1962 to 1972 witnessed the printing and distribution of additional primary school textbooks that had been translated and adopted from a series produced in English. As the need to improve educational services increased, new ideas such as educational study programs and the establishment of publication organizations began to appear. In 1972 for instance, the creation of a Department of Educational Services was proposed. This eventually led to the Division of Curriculum and Teaching Materials Production in 1973, which was the forerunner of two current organizations—the Institute of Curriculum Development and Research and the Educational Materials Production and Distribution Agency (EMPDA). This was an important step for the development of textbook publication in the country. The responsibilities of these two agencies were to write, translate, produce, print, and distribute textbooks under the Ministry of Education. The EMPDA was initially regarded as a manufacturing and distribution organization, participating in other tasks of the Ministry of Education. Its publishing function is a recent development. Until the early 1980s, manuscripts were created and sent to print, by and large, without the benefits of a professional publisher. The foundation of the educational publishing house replaced the author-to-printer arrangement.

By 1993/94, the number of titles printed by the EMPDA had reached 972, but the cost was heavily subsidized by international loans and assistance. The agency's production plan for 1995/96 indicated more than 9.5 million, of which 77.5 percent was to be accomplished by its own printing plant.[12] As the demand for textbooks increases, the agency is continuously facing shortages of resources and capacity.

Current Conditions in the Publishing Environment

As Ethiopia emerges from war, famine, and underdevelopment, there has not been much progress in private, local publishing, which suffered significantly from the domination of the state monopoly, censorship, and unfavorable political and economic conditions. The country is still short of private publishers to address the needs of independent writers and readers whose numbers are growing as a result of the current democratization and liberalized economic policy. More than twenty small and medium-sized private printing presses and four publishing houses operate in the capital today, but there are few printers outside Addis Ababa. Five of the largest printing houses are operated by the government. There is a university printing press to cater to publication needs at the tertiary level.

From 1978 to 1992, a total of 79 titles were published by the two largest publishers, Kuraz and the Ethiopian Book Center. These books included fiction, general topics, and educational materials. Translated books, mainly fiction, dominate the small book trade that exists outside of educational publishing. Research indicates that from 1986 to 1994, a total of 150 new titles were recorded. Children's books are beginning to appear also. The Educational Publishing Agency under the Ministry of Education has been able to produce children's books with support from UNICEF. Over 20 new titles of creative writing have been published so far.[13] Since 1992, books have been published in several languages other than Amharic and English. Books that could not be printed before were published as a result of the new press law. New titles of fiction were produced in the Gurage and Oromya languages; 98 new editions and translated publications were produced in Tigrai language as well.[14] Other translations are in process in other local languages. Books of foreign origin are reprinted also. Reference, academic, and professional publications dominate imported books.

Liberalization and the Move Away from Public Monopoly

The economic reform program has attempted to create the necessary conditions for the development of a market economy, with increased participation from the private sector. A privatization scheme was introduced to expedite the withdrawal of the state from specific economic activities that need to be managed by the private sector.[15] Many enterprises that used to operate under the state are being transferred to private owners. An agency has been operating both at the central and regional levels to facilitate the transfer to private ownership.

Conditions have been created to encourage local and outside investors to participate. Incentives, investment guarantees, and certain protections have facilitated individual and joint investment ventures in most economic sectors without any limitation of capital.[16] The book development and publishing sector is one beneficiary of these developments.

In today's Ethiopia, press freedom is guaranteed by law. The law specifically prohibits censorship. In 1994, a press licensing department was established to implement the law. From the time the law was enacted until March 1995, 251 private organizations and individuals have been given press licenses to operate as publishers of periodicals, magazines, and newspapers.[17] Furthermore, private publishers and printers have introduced new practices in advertising and circulation. The circulation of new materials has increased with new outlets for sales. A range of private and government publications and periodicals are sold in the streets and roads. The number and scope of private publications are gradually expanding as the new press law is put into practice. A professional association of journalists operates in Ethiopia today. There is a training center in the capital for journalists. The government press prepares, publishes, and distributes government newspapers, magazines, and various publications in different languages. The ultimate aim, however, is to transfer government mass media, step by step, to private ownership.[18]

The New Language Policy

Ethiopia is a multilingual country. More than eighty languages are spoken. Amharic was declared an official language in the 1955 constitution. Other major local languages include Tigrai, Otomya, Sidama, Hadya, Gedeo, Kambata, Somali, and Afar. An Academy of Ethiopian Languages was established in 1942 (with the foundation of the Ministry of Education and Fine Arts) to promote indigenous languages. The academy supports language study and research in the areas of linguistics, lexicography, terminology, translation and oral literature.[19]

Today, each nation/nationality has the right of promoting its culture and history, using and developing its own language, and in general, of administering its own affairs within its territory. Amharic and English continue to be used as official languages on the national level. Today, more than eleven national languages are used as mediums of instruction at the primary level. English and Amharic are used as mediums of instruction or are taught as foreign languages. The publication of books in different languages presents special problems. Print runs of educational materials have decreased. Printing primary level textbooks in different languages is not viable for the private publisher. As a result, books are not printed in all languages.

The Need for a Book Policy

Publishing has immense cultural and economic importance for a country like Ethiopia. As an industry and business, local book publishing would help to create job opportunities, develop human and natural resources and culture, save foreign exchange, and produce and make books more available in accordance with the needs of the country. However, indigenous publishing faces unique problems.

A book is a national resource. It should be treated as an integral part of the cultural and educational policy of a country. A national book policy setting standards and specifications would serve as a useful guide for publishers and printers. A book policy would contribute to publishing decisions, plans, and production. It would help to produce books in accordance with a required standard and guarantee a better supply of cheap, good-quality books and alleviate the continuous scarcity of books in the country. Therefore a book policy that serves as an umbrella for all publishing activities needs to be put into practice.

Many challenges still face this nascent industry. Skilled manpower at all levels of publishing process is needed urgently. Book production can only become a reality with experienced and skilled writers, illustrators, editors, book designers, production experts, and booksellers. Not all publishers and printers are equipped with appropriate facilities and modern technology. There is a shortage of spare parts and consumables. Printing presses are old and uneconomical to operate. Production activities are often hampered by equipment failure, coupled with a lack of maintenance personnel. Few publishers and printers use modern technology that would save time and scant resources. The use of desktop publishing for writing, editing, and designing is a new development introduced just recently and still practiced by few. Color reproduction facilities are scarce. All this has affected the operation of local publishers and printers. Due to lack of appropriate facilities and equipment, therefore, the quality that book publishers are able to produce is low and prices are relatively high for consumers who are not in a position to sustain this market.

Lack of financing mechanisms for the purchase of modern equipment to support book publishing is a major area of concern for indigenous enterprises. Operating in a poor business environment, facing high interest rates, high taxes on imported goods (raw materials, spare parts, consumables, and machinery), and high maintenance costs have worsened conditions. As most private publishers have no financial assets, creditors (especially banks) are reluctant to extend loans. As a result, their share of book production is small amounting to only 5 percent.[20] Local and international funds should be made available to commercial indigenous publishers, in order to improve the situation.

Without credit or resources, local commercial publishers, printers, and booksellers face impossible competition from their state-owned counterparts. The state remains the main publisher, printer, and distributor of books; it owns five of the biggest printers, and the only educational publishing and distribution enterprise in the capital. Private writers, publishers, printers, and distributors continue to have limited access to the market of educational publishing or to outside assistance.

Challenges Facing Local Writers

Though the number of writers has increased in the past few years, the problems they face are enormous. They suffer from a lack of experienced publishers to help them produce readable and salable books. Recent findings indicate that there are many writers holding collections of unpublished manuscripts due to the lack of publishing outlets. Those who get their manuscripts printed must deal directly with printers (usuallly government owned) and face inflexible rules and directives. They have few options. They cannot get books printed without advance payment, and they are obliged to store books afterwards. In the absence of competent booksellers and bookshops, writers are forced to sell books on their own, book by book, and from place to place looking for buyers. Usually writers find few customers able or willing to pay the high price that must be assigned to new books. Though the royalty paid to writers amounts to between 10 and 12 percent, it is hard to tell whether their share was fair or not compared to the earnings of publishers and printers. Besides not being able to enjoy the advantages of an established publishing industry, most writers have little understanding or knowledge of editorial, design, production, and printing processes. As a result they are not always able to make the best decisions. Few guides for writing or translating books exist in the country. The training programs conducted so far (with the benefit of outside assistance) focus on in-house textbook writers, editors, and designers of government institutions. Outsiders from the commercial sector have little access to such programs.

Access to Books

Circulation of books is limited in the country. The reader outside the capital has limited access to books and other publications. A poor infrastructure (poor roads and communication), accompanied by the absence of commercial networks of local book traders, has contributed to the difficulty of delivering books to readers all over the country. Publishers producing books other than textbooks have limited markets available to them. Due to high prices, few readers can afford to buy books. In general the low literacy rate and the poor socioeconomic condition of the country limit the potential of the market. The situation is further complicated by the lack of distribution channels and marketing. There are few bookshops in the country; they continue to be concentrated in the capital. Books and other publications of general reading and information continue to be rare. Distribution of textbooks is centralized. An agency of the Ministry of Education is responsible for distribution of school books to the regions. Each region then takes the responsibility of making books available to schools. The system of textbook distribution as a whole is inadequate and inefficient. There is a serious problem of making books available in accordance with school schedules. Though the official pupil book ratio is 2:1 it is estimated to be higher.[21]

Library service has continuously deteriorated. Community libraries centered in the capital and regional towns were built many years ago and need to be expanded. They lack recently published materials. School libraries lack current materials as well. There has been no library improvement for many years. Library service encourages children and the community to read and write, and enhances education and training. Conditions need to be improved.

Schemes to develop publishing in areas like children's books are nonexistent. The funds contributed by international assistance agencies and the government for publishing have been (for the most part) limited to textbook production. In order to encourage the growth of literacy (and social development, as a whole) new schemes are necessary.

The Paradox of State Involvement

Textbook publishing represents a high growth area in Ethiopia than other types of publications. The state promoted the idea and practice of institutionalized textbook publishing as a means of implementing its educational policy in the country beginning in the second half of this century. Unfortunately, though, private printers only participate in the production of textbooks when the workload of the state's textbook printing house is beyond its capacity.

There are conflicting views as to the virtues of state involvement. In general, publishing seems to function better without government control, due to the inflexible organizational framework that controls government bodies; activities are controlled by state laws and regulation, and they are more subject to political influence. Centralized manuscript preparation and textbook production have contributed to low quality. State involvement has been characterized by inadequate planning and a disproportionate allocation of resources toward textbooks. Moreover, the publishing industry is not well understood by government authorities and generally suffers a low profile, as in most developing countries. Operating without an absolute state monopoly of textbooks would no doubt contribute to the development of independent educational publishing companies in Ethiopia. Nevertheless, the participation of the state remains important and desirable since it has the means to maintain and coordinate activities until local commercial publishers are strengthened. It takes time until the values of the curriculum and textbooks are understood by indigenous and commercial publishers so that problems do not occur as a result of too much emphasis on profit at the expense of educational welfare.

However, in the long run, there is no alternative to the indigenization and commercialization of the book industry. A strategy to address the concerns and interests of the state should be established to guide the gradual replacement of the current public monopoly in favor of a private sector. The following are some of the points that can accelerate the process.

1. *Concentrate on policy issues related to book development only.*

Under the present circumstances, the responsibility for educational services should remain with the state. The main question, however, is not who is responsible, but rather how best to delegate this responsibility so as to achieve the objectives of the national education policy. Certain activities of textbook publishing might be better implemented by the private sector. What is needed is a clear policy to serve as a guide for operations and the transfer of publishing activities to the private sector step by step. A carefully conceived operational strategy (based on national priorities) is necessary, though. One way to achieve this goal would be involving commercial publishers in the production of textbooks in different local languages. Obstacles that prohibit publishers and printers from competing with the state should be lifted. They should be able to publish, print, and distribute materials for school use working directly with the state at the central and regional level. This could result in the availability of new materials in the schools. Production, distribution, and availability of textbooks and other educational materials could be improved also. The central and regional states should remain the sole purchasers and facilitators in textbook provision, however, until alternatives are found in the future.

The decentralized administration of the country and autonomy of regions has made decentralization of book supply and private distribution of books a possibility. Ways to ease the burden of government expenditure should be found by gradually introducing cost-sharing methods. The existing book rental system has already proven to be a good method. The practice of selling and buying supplementary materials at schools and bookshops will encourage privatization.

2. *Introduce book development schemes for entrepreneurs.*

There is no writer, publisher, printer, or bookseller in Ethiopia with the necessary capital and human resources to establish and run his or her publishing enterprise without outside help. Increased funding for publishing would also encourage more local writers to produce manuscripts. Incentives for writers and library services support programs should be encouraged. To meet the challenges of limited manpower resources, training for writers, translators, publishers, designers, editors, production experts, printers, and booksellers, etc. in the public and private sectors should be made a national priority. The integrated efforts of national publishers associations, international assistance, and the government are indispensable in the implementation of such initiatives. The government's role both in Addis Ababa and the regions could be managed through book development councils. These book development councils could facilitate privatization and coordinate the interests of the smaller nations/nationalities with those of the country at large.

3. *Encourage projects related to publishing.*

The government is currently preoccupied with other priorities.

As a result, the indigenous publisher has not yet been lucky enough to enjoy the benefits of its attention. Reduction of customs duties and taxes on imported goods, income tax exemptions, improvements in techniques and forms of organization, credit to expand activities and become competitive, new investment regulations (particularly for writers, publishers, printers, and booksellers, etc.) are necessary to change the competitive balance in favor of the private sector.

4. *Initiate research programs.*
Research projects to determine the best means of developing indigenous publishing houses may contribute to the creation of an effective publishing model that can function in harmony with the new competitive, free market economy. Such initiatives could assist in viewing problems from a variety of perspectives and to deter people from rushing to adopt outside models.

Pertinent Issues Ahead
Ethiopia is currently undergoing fundamental socioeconomic and political changes. It is adopting policies of reform to guide the transition from a planned economy to a free market economy. Books and printed material are necessary to human progress in general and to the development of a democratic society, in particular. Past means of book production need to be adjusted according to the new realities of competition and the freedom to write without the restrictions of ideology. All past generations of authors, publishers, and printers of the planned economic system have to be reoriented according to the principles of a free market economy; publishers have to learn new ways and practices for reaching consumers.

The private publishing sector has enormous potential for development. It has the dynamism and the motivation to develop expertise. But it also faces challenges and constraints that result from an environment long controlled by a public agency. A low standard of living and illiteracy remain the main obstacles to successful marketing. The subsidy system of financing government activities continues to function and will not change quickly in light of the grave consequences that it might have on disadvantaged areas and sectors of population. Consumer subsidies need to be encouraged to balance the effects of rising prices and in order to encourage readers to buy books. But this needs to be done without an inhibiting the development of a competitive publishing industry. Financial assistance should be targeted to purchaser's needs to the extent that the investment will benefit the industry as a whole.

The extent to which old ideology has governed local industry and business cannot be underestimated. Suspicion, doubt, and reluctance are common problems of cooperation and hinder joint efforts to improve the situation. With the introduction of competition, greater choice for consumers, and improvements in the standard of production, better availability of written materials can be achieved. Privatizing state holdings would facilitate this process. Among the potential forces that will contribute to the success of indigenous publishing development are professionals in the publishing process, publishing houses, the public at large, the state, and international assistance. The importance of coordinating the interests of publishers, authors, and readers should be well understood by all parties.

The role of the publisher cannot be trivialized. The existing publishing structure and method should be improved with the active participation of new publishers. Publishers associations can serve common interests of the publishing industry. Authors and the public (readers) should play an important role in strengthening indigenous publishing to secure better services. State and donor support should be directed to the needs of publishing as a whole, rather than to specific interests, as the book remains a central piece of cultural and educational life. Furthermore, there are areas of concern in which the forces mentioned above could work together.

The existence of a literate population is an essential prerequisite in order for publishing to develop. It serves as a source of both authors and consumers. Children represent the majority of the population, and it is to their advantage for local publishing to grow.

In an environment where the rate of production of new editions is small, translation of books continue to play an important role. The role of bookshops should be properly appreciated. They are an important link between publishers and readers. They need to be organized, located, and programmed according to the needs and interests of customers. Their services should not be limited to the major populations centers only; other sectors of society need to be reached through different means. Distribution of books cannot be concentrated only in the capital and regional cities. Decentralization from the majors cities to the regions is essential A concerted effort is required to strengthen viable commercial distribution networks throughout the country. Recent events have opened a more favorable environment for book publishing. Its future is not dependent on privatization alone. The strategic involvement of the state and aid agencies is essential. It is hoped that the government and international assistance will serve as a catalyst to accelerate present activities toward the sustainable development of the publishing industry.

Notes

1. Transitional Government of Ethiopia, *Education Sector Strategy* (Addis Ababa: Transitional Government of Ethiopia, 1994), 18–19.
2. *Population Education Newsletter* no. 9 (1996): 15.
3. *The World of Education* 14 (1995): 67.
4. Ibid., 69
5. "Exhibition of Ethiopian Manuscripts from the Collection of the Institute of Ethiopian Studies" *Journal of Ethiopian Studies* (1988): 9–10.
6. *Voice of the Ministry of Information* 1, no.1 (March 1995): 31–35.
7. Ibid.
8. Ibid.
9. *Production Technical Specification Manual* (Kuraz Publishing House, n.d.), 2.
10. *Voice of The Ministry Of Information* 1, no. 1 (March 1995): 32–33.
11. Ministry of Education. *Sector Study of Ethiopian Education*, vol. 1 (Addis Ababa: Ministry of Education, 1983), 1–23.
12. *1995/96 Yearly Plan* (Educational Materials Production and Distribution Agency, 1995), 2.
13. Zerihun Asfaw, *The Situation of Ethiopian Literature: A Short Overview, 1958–1993*, 1–29.
14. Ibid.
15. Privatization Act of 1994.
16. *Voice of the Ministry of Information* 1, no. 2 (August 1995): 23–25.
17. *View Of Government Mass Media*,May 1995, 6.
18. Ibid., 14–16.
19. *Facts and Figures*, Academy of Ethiopian Languages, June 1986.
20. Asfaw Damte, *The Role of the State in Book Production and Distribution* (1993) p. 9.
21. This information was obtained from the discussion with regional curriculum personnel.

5

Privatization in Publishing: the Zambian Experience

RAY MUNAMWIMBU

Zambia is a relatively small country of 9.4 million people, landlocked but rich in mineral resources. In the multiparty elections in 1991 the long-established government of Dr. Kenneth Kaunda was ousted. The previous regime's centralized control is now being liberalized, and parastatal companies are opening to competition. This is true of publishing as well as other industries. Zambia is not simply hungry for books: it is starved for them.

Zambia's publishing history dates back to 1937, when the African Literature Committee of Northern Rhodesia was established. In 1948 this committee became part of the Joint Northern Rhodesia and Nyasaland Publications Bureau, which operated under the auspices of the Department of African Education. In 1964 when Zambia became independent the bureau became a separate entity known as the Zambia Publications Bureau. Its major task was to produce books and encourage black Zambians to read and write. The bureau also sponsored essay and novel writing competitions as one way of stimulating an interest in writing among black Zambians as well as a means of getting publishable manuscripts.

A few years after independence the Zambian government introduced the policy of nationalization in pursuit of economic independence. For the book industry, this policy led to the establishment of the Kenneth Kaunda Foundation (KKF) in 1966. The KKF was mandated to publish, market, and distribute educational books. In order for the KKF to execute these functions effectively, it formed two subsidiary companies: a publishing company, the National Educational Company of Zambia, in 1967; and a marketing and distribution company, the National Educational and Distribution Company of Zambia, in 1968.

With the newly established KKF in full operation, the Zambia Publications Bureau became irrelevant and went into voluntary liquidation in 1969. In 1971 the KKF became a statutory corporation through an Act of Parliament. At the time of the establishment of the KKF, several multinational publishing companies were present in the country—Oxford University Press, Longman, and Heinemann Educational books. However, these multinational publishers were compelled to wind up their business in Zambia because all manuscripts for educational textbooks prepared, tested, and revised by the Curriculum Development Centre of the Ministry of Education were submitted to the KKF for publication and sale to schools. The primary school market was (effectively) wrestled away from the multinational publishers. The multinational publishers in Zambia found the return on their activities to be uneconomical and complicated further by difficulties in converting foreign exchange.

The presence of the multinational publishing companies until that time had not helped to advance the local publishing industry. The manuscripts developed by the multinational publishers were typically edited, designed, and typeset in the publisher's metropolitan headquarters. The camera-ready copies were then printed in countries outside of Zambia—such as Singapore, Hong Kong, and South Africa, where printing costs were considerably lower. This meant that the printed books were merely shipped to Zambia for sale. This method of getting books produced and printed did not benefit Zambia because the printing infrastructure in the country remained undeveloped. Similarly, book publishing skills remained in the formative stages.

The departure of the multinational publishing companies resulted in a mandate from the Zambian government to the KKF to undertake book publishing, printing, bookselling, and distribution countrywide. These functions should have been performed by four different companies. This multiplicity of functions eventually overburdened the KKF and rendered the whole setup ineffective and inefficient.

This arrangement also left very little or no room for the private entrepreneur to operate successfully in publishing or bookselling. The Curriculum Development Centre of the Ministry of Education continued to submit all of its manuscripts to the KKF for publication. The foundation held a monopoly in the production and supply of educational books and school supplies; payment for orders was made centrally by the Ministry of Education.

The departure of the multinational publishing companies signified the demise of private-sector publishing to the benefit of the parastatal publishing sector, or so it appeared initially. In the late 1960s and early 1970s, when the national economy was sound, the KKF managed to publish an average of 100 (75 educational titles and visual aids and 25 general titles) per year up to 1975. The print runs for textbooks ranged between 3,000 and 120,000 copies of teachers' handbooks and pupils' books respectively, which at that time almost satisfied the school population. For general titles the print runs ranged from 2,000 to 5,000 copies per title.

The availability of funds for educational materials from the national budget enabled the KKF to publish the large number of titles. When the national economy declined during the post-1975 era the budgetary allocation for student needs also dropped in real terms. This adversely affected the performance of the KKF as the "national" publisher. It was at this point that the burden of the multiplicity of functions took its toll on the foundation and rendered the whole setup incapable of fulfilling the nation's needs.

Development Assistance

The vulnerability of a system where the supply of textbooks is dependent on state funding and a single publisher became obvious in 1979 when stocks completely ran out and there was no alternative source. It was at this point that the KKF approached the government of Finland for development aid funds for the purpose of reprinting the Zambia Primary Course books in Finland. The collaboration with the Finnish government resulted in the Zambia Educational Materials Project (ZEMP). The ZEMP contained two phases:

• rehabilitation through the immediate reprinting of core Zambia Primary Course textbooks in Finland to supply Zambian primary schools and
• development of new textbooks in selected subjects for the Zambian secondary schools, the development of editorial capacity at the KKF as well as the systematic development of the KKF as a sound publishing, printing, and distribution company.

The ZEMP program took off in 1984. The project put some new life into the KKF and the Curriculum Development Centre. Until 1991 the two institutions were the only ones supported by the ZEMP. Subsequently, ZEMP had to channel its support to the educational sector through the Ministry of Education Procurement and Supplies Unit for other companies to benefit as well. This continued until the end of the last phase of the project in December 1995.

Apart from the KKF, two other parastatal companies were established: Printpak Zambia Limited and Zambia Printing Company Limited. The two organizations operated under the Companies Act and functioned under the auspices of the Ministry of Information and Broadcasting Services. Until 1988 both companies were in the business of printing newspapers, commercial stationery, and books, including books for the KKF. In 1988 the two companies established book publishing departments. This was after realizing that the KKF had failed to meet the demand for educational books even after getting support from the Finnish International Development Agency (FINNIDA) through ZEMP. However, the two companies did not have access to manuscripts developed by the Curriculum Development Centre. The manuscripts from this source were a preserve of the KKF. The two companies had to commission authors to write manuscripts for textbooks (in the case of Printpak Zambia Limited) and for children's books (in the case of Zambia Printing Company).

In spite of the hostile environment for the publishing industry at the time, a few private publishing houses emerged. Notable among these were Primrose Publishing House, Apple Books Publications, Bookworld Publishing House, and Multimedia Zambia Limited. These operated side by side with the three parastatal companies in the mid-1980s. Except for Multimedia Zambia, however, the rest of the companies faded into oblivion as they could not withstand the cut-throat competition with parastatal companies, especially the KKF, which not only enjoyed government support but were exempt from any form of taxation.

Liberalization
While Zambia's economy was declining, the KKF—with only limited capacity and inadequate skills for a thriving book industry—failed to meet the growing demand for both educational and general books. The foregoing reasons and lack of competition from private-sector publishing contributed greatly to the decline of the book industry in the period up to 1991. It therefore did not come as a surprise when the Movement for Multiparty Democracy government liberalized the production and supply of educational materials on November 15, 1991 and changed the name of the KKF to the Zambia Educational Publish-

ing House (ZEPH). Although the press release from the Ministry of Education proclaiming the liberalization of the production and supply of educational materials was not followed by a detailed plan, a number of positive developments have since taken place. The liberalization has stimulated a growing interest in book publishing and bookselling among both local and foreign companies.

The book industry has witnessed the return of such multinational publishing companies as Longman, Oxford University Press, and Macmillan Publishers, hopefully a signal for a brighter future for the country's book industry. In addition, a few private publishing companies have emerged locally following the creation of this new environment. By March 1993, there were forty-two publishers registered with the Booksellers and Publishers Association of Zambia. In spite of the seemingly large numbers, however, there were only six notable local publishing houses, the newest ones being School and College Press and Yorvik Publishing Company. The local publishing scene at this point in time was still dominated by the multinational publishers. It should be noted, however, that multinational publishers have still not invested fully in Zambia by developing a complete publishing infrastructure locally. At present, Zambia is still being used as a market for books produced elsewhere, although the nation aspires to have an indigenous book industry. The return of multinational publishers should (ideally) transfer publishing skills and technology from the developed countries to Zambia.

The policy of liberalization has set the pace for privatization by creating an enabling environment for the emergence of private-sector publishing initiatives. Currently, there are fifteen active publishers registered with the Booksellers and Publishers Association of Zambia. (See Appendix A.) Out of this number there are three state-owned publishers: Times Printpak Zambia Limited, Zambia Printing Company Limited, and ZEPH. Of the three state-owned publishing companies, only ZEPH has been earmarked for privatization during the 1996/97 period by the Zambia Privatization Agency. The remaining twelve publishing companies are privately owned. These include the three multinational publishers (Longman Zambia Limited, Oxford University Press, and Macmillan Publishers Zambia Limited) and four that have been formed since the liberalization of the production and supply of educational materials in 1991.

The policy of liberalization for publishing meant that ZEPH would no longer enjoy a monopoly for the production and supply of school books. It would have to compete with other publishers in the newly opened market. It must be noted that the largest book buyer in Zambia presently is the Ministry of Education, which buys school books for more than 3,800 primary schools with 1.7 million pupils and about 612 secondary schools with 250,000 pupils. The educational establishment has been without sufficient new books for the past seventeen years. As a result, the current book-to-pupil ratios for course books (1:2 for grades 1–7 and 1:1 for grades 8–12) are rarely fulfilled. The same is true for supplementary readers, where the book-to-pupil ratio is 1:5 for all grades.[1] This deficit is being redressed through substantial programs of foreign aid. This aid is channeled through the Ministry of Education Procurement and Supplies Unit. The donor agencies involved in the funding of textbook provision are FINNIDA, the Swedish International Development Authority, the Overseas Development Agency, the European Community, UNICEF, as well as lending institutions such as the World Bank.

Competition and Decentralization

In order to even the playground for publishers operating in Zambia, the Ministry of Education (through the Procurement and Supplies Unit) has adopted a policy of tendering local publication of school books that are currently being prepared within the Curriculum Development Centre. Interested publishers, including ZEPH, have to submit competitive bids and the successful publishers are awarded the contracts.

The current tendering system and substantial foreign aid in the educational sector have encouraged the establishment of private publishing companies because of good business opportunities. To this end it is anticipated that a few more private entrepreneurs will rise to the occasion and participate in the book publishing business. In real terms, therefore, privatization in Zambian publishing will consist more of the formation of new private publishing companies as there are only three state-owned publishing houses to be privatized.

The foregoing scenario involves publishing exclusively of school books in English, the national language and until now the national language of instruction. The Ministry of Education now plans to begin instruction in the first three grades in local languages, teaching English at that level only as a second language. This policy, if pursued actively, will expand the school book market further since it will create more and new publishing opportunities in the seven major vernacular languages.

One worrying factor, however, is that there has been too much emphasis on publishing school books (for the obvious reason that there is a ready market and available money) at the expense of general reading books that are sold through the bookstores. It is worth mentioning here that the procurement system for school books to date is still centralized. In other words all book purchases are centrally made at Ministry of Education headquarters. There are, however, plans to decentralize the procurement system, with the establishment of school management boards. The current system of procurement "killed" the initiative of opening bookshops in several parts of the country. These bookshops would also stock general titles in English and the seven major Zambian Languages.

The absence of private bookshops in many parts of the country has compelled existing publishers to concentrate more on textbook publishing than publishing general titles. This is because they are able to sell textbooks directly to the Ministry of Education, without depending on the scant network of bookshops through which they would sell general titles. There are presently ten booksellers (see Appendix B)—among which ZEPH has the widest coverage, with eleven bookshops dotted across the country. The remaining nine booksellers (all of them private) have their bookshops situated in urban areas, mostly in Zambia's major cities. With the impending decentralization of schoolbook purchasing to school management boards, it is anticipated that a few additional private bookshops will be opened in other parts of the country to sell both textbooks and general titles.

Unmet Market Potential
Between 1985 and January 1995 a total of 750 titles were published by the fifteen listed publishers.[2] Of these 750 titles, 373 are categorized as general titles (fiction, sociocultural, and children's books), 124 as religious titles, and 254 as school books. Of the 750 titles, 502 were in English, while the balance were in the various local languages (see Appendix C). In a country that has an estimated population of 9.4 million, the total of 750 titles published over a period of ten years by fifteen publishers highlights the underdevelopment of local book publishing and the extent to which the market's potential remains unexploited.[3] Another conclusion that can be drawn is that publishing

in the Zambian languages has additional potential for expansion as so few titles have been published in these languages. This is complicated at present by the lack of skilled translators capable of translating books into a Zambian language or vice-versa.

The foregoing scenario clearly demonstrates that there exists a lot of potential in the book publishing business. What might be lacking perhaps is the existence of a better environment in which all the stakeholders might play their roles effectively, with a view to making publishing a thriving business.

Privatization

Privatization is a process whereby government divests it shareholding in the parastatal sector. This action limits the scope of political interference in decision making and increases managerial incentives by making managers responsible to shareholders who are more capable of monitoring the performance of their business better than are government officials. The main objectives of privatization are:
- to create a commercial environment in all business enterprises;
- to stimulate public participation in business enterprises;
- to stimulate cooperation in all business sectors;
- to generate funds for investment where companies are sold for cash;
- to reduce government budgetary obligations in situations where operations of parastatal companies are subsidized; and
- to reduce government involvement in business.

From the foregoing objectives it is clear that Zambia's economic future lies in private-sector development, which is the basis for economic growth.

Performance of Private Firms

Most private firms are performing much better than are the parastatal bodies. The main factor is that the work culture in private firms is commercially oriented. Appointments to key managerial positions are made on merit in private firms and not on patronage, as is the case in most parastatal companies. The organizational structure for a private firm is carefully tailored to suit the volume of the undertaking and is devoid of unnecessary overheads, as occur frequently in parastatal enterprises. Efficiency is the key word for private firms. The newly established private publishing firms, despite the fact that they are new, are already performing much better than the three parastatal publishing houses in terms of the quality of their products and in meeting delivery deadlines. They market their books through ZEPH and some well-established private bookshops.

These private publishers have their books printed outside Zambia, either in Zimbabwe or South Africa, where printing costs are reasonable. For instance, it is almost 50 percent cheaper to print a book in South Africa than in Zambia. One reason for this is that printed books come into the country duty-free. For local printing, paper has to be imported with a 15 percent duty as well as a 5 percent Import Declaration Fee for any purchase above U.S.$500. This is compounded by the expensive spare parts for the printing machines that have to be imported. The printer has to pay duty and VAT on the import of these spares. These factors make local printing costs high and uncompetitive.

Private publishing firms depend on hired editors. Most editors work for parastatal publishing houses: ZEPH employs twelve editors who are specialized in various fields; Zambia Publishing Company has one editor and Printpak Zambia employs three editors, two of whom were former ZEPH staff members. This cadre of editors is competent, experienced, and properly trained in terms of editorial skills. ZEMP sponsored and conducted a series of editorial skills workshops for ZEPH editors.

Capitalization has been one of the teething problems facing emergent private publishers and the well-established companies as well. There is in most cases insufficient working capital. The only recourse has been to get loans from commercial banks at very high interest rates. The Ministry of Education in very exceptional cases pays a downpayment, especially to emergent private publishers, who get contracts to print textbooks tendered by the ministry.

Toward a National Policy

An attempt to create a favorable environment for expansion was made in January 1995, when the Ministry of Education in collaboration with the Booksellers and Publishers Association of Zambia organized a seminar on educational book distribution and marketing. The major purpose of the gathering was to bring together all the major players in the book industry and review the impact of the policy of liberalization and the performance of the book industry in a free-market economy. The seminar was well attended by all the stakeholders (see

Appendix D). The general observation was that while a lot had been achieved since 1991 when the government implemented the policy of liberalization, there were still some misunderstandings of the manner in which some stakeholders played their roles that, if unchecked, would impede the growth of the publishing business in the liberalized climate.

Three major issues arose out of the deliberations, and these were: book development, bookselling, and procurement. After a lot of debate it was agreed that the Curriculum Development Centre should concentrate on preparing syllabuses, curriculum development and research, and approving books for use in schools. The center should surrender the role of developing books to publishers. In order to promote the bookselling business, it was agreed that all publishers should market their books (including textbooks) through booksellers. It was also agreed that in order to facilitate the formation of bookshops in various parts of the country, the Ministry of Education should decentralize funding for the purchase of school books.

It is, however, disheartening to learn that after one year very little progress has been made in implementing these recommendations. The Curriculum Development Centre has continued to develop books using subject specialists. This arrangement will make it difficult to forestall partisan professional interests on the part of the specialists which may impede the approval of deserving textbooks presented for evaluation and approval by the publishers. With regard to bookselling, some publishers have continued to sell their books directly to customers within the same locality of the private bookshops that have the same books to sell, thereby creating unfair competition. The Ministry of Education still purchases books centrally, making it unprofitable for booksellers to open up bookshops in other parts of the country.

The underlying reason for nonconformity with regard to some of these agreements by certain of the key players in the book industry is that there is no watchdog. There is at present no official government policy or legislation to regulate and supervise the functions of various stakeholders in the book industry. The Zambian government, apart from proclaiming the policy of liberalization, has not yet codified a national book policy. This may explain the omission from the various National Development Plans of any mention of a comprehensive book development program. The book development program in this context would be seen as a framework for the systematic growth and enhancement of different aspects of Zambia's book industry.[4]

A national book development plan once formulated would forestall ad hoc decisions being taken on matters affecting the book industry in the country. Additionally, a legislative framework would provide for clearly articulated procedural machinery for issues such as taxes and tariffs on imported raw materials and books; remittance of royalties or reprint fees; application of international conventions such as the Florence Agreement and its protocol; and development funding for the book industry as a deliberate effort to enhance its contribution to national development.

It is, however, pleasing to note that a task force has since been appointed to formulate a national book policy and establish the National Book Development Council. To this end a lot of work has been done and a draft document will shortly be presented to a national symposium for debate. This is a step in the right direction as it will foster the growth of the private publishing sector. The council will be able to regulate and supervise the process of book development in an integrated and coherent manner. It will also be in a position to lobby for reasonable taxes and tariffs on imported raw materials such as printing paper and other inputs.

Against all these odds, however, the liberalization of the production and supply of textbooks and the government's commitment to supply schools with sufficient books provide a good environment and impetus for the systematic development of a private local book industry. It is, however, crucially important to enhance this new policy and environment by introducing well-defined modus operandi for publishers, booksellers and printers. In addition there should be in place (initially) deliberate mechanisms to help emerging local publishers to establish themselves. For instance, the Ministry of Education Procurement and Supplies Unit, through its tendering system, could give sizable publishing jobs to emerging publishers and partially fund the execution of such jobs. It is also worth mentioning that about 60 percent of Zambia's population of 9.4 million is under sixteen years of age. This community deserves books produced locally that are related to national experiences and the local environment.

A healthy book trade is essential for encouraging literacy outside the school. The literacy rate in Zambia is still a source of concern (see Appendix E). A strong local publishing industry is equally essential to the development of an understanding of local history, society, and culture.

Privatization in publishing will no doubt encourage entrepreneurs to invest in the publishing business since there will be an even playground and free competition. In the next two to three years, it is very likely that the remaining two parastatal publishing houses will be privatized as well. The two companies do not actually pose a threat to private publishers like ZEPH does. To date, ZEPH still has an upper hand in publishing, printing, distribution, and marketing because of the investment put into it before 1991 in the form of donated printing machines and commercial trucks.

It is, however, encouraging to note that after five years of liberalization, there is a tremendous response from individuals and companies to establish private publishing houses. This trend is likely to continue, but at a slow pace largely because of two principal impediments to publishing development in Zambia—lack of capital in an economy suffering from high inflation and a lack of publishing expertise within the local society.

It must, however, be acknowledged that the policy favoring a free-market economy by the present government offers good investment opportunities and a conducive environment for a thriving book publishing business. In conclusion, the book industry in Zambia has entered a new era that is full of challenges. The rules of the game have already been set. What is needed now is for the National Book Development Council to play the role of umpire in this nascent publishing industry.

Notes

1. Martin Ferns, *Report on National Seminar on the Educational Book Trade, Distribution and Marketing in Zambia*, (Coordinator, Zambia Educational Materials Project, 1995).
2. Hudwell Mwacalimba and Christine Kanyengo, *Zambian Books in Print and ISBN Publishers Directory*,(Lusaka: Booksellers and Publishers Association of Zambia, 1995).
3. Report by United Nations Population Fund in 1995.
4. Katongo A. Chali and Chris H. Chirwa, *A Study on Textbook Provision in Zambia and Feasibility of Cooperation among SADC Countries* (UNESCO).

Appendix A
List of Active Publishers Registered with BPAZ

Name	Status
1. Zambia Educational Publishing House	government owned
2. Zambia Printing Company Limited	government owned
3. Times Printpak Zambia Limited	government owned
4. Multimedia Zambia	private
5. Maiden Publishing House	private
6. Macmillan Zambia Limited	private
7. Yorvik Publishing Company Limited	private
8. School and College Press	private
9. Longman Zambia Limited	private
10. Oxford University Press	private
11. Apple Books Publishers	private
12. Bookworld Publishers	private
13. University of Zambia Press	private
14. Primrose Publishers Limited	private
15. Baptist Publishing House	private

Appendix B
List of Existing Booksellers In Zambia

Name	No. of Bookshops	Location
1. Zambia Educational Publishing House	11	rural/urban
2. Bookworld	2	urban
3. University Bookshop	2	urban
4. Cookie's Bookshop	1	urban
5. Pages and Things	1	urban
6. Excel Zambia Limited	1	urban
7. Maiden Bookshop	1	urban
8. Jamas Bookshop	1	urban
9. Printpak Bookshop	1	urban
10. Afro Educational Services	1	urban

Appendix C
Book Publishing in Zambia, by Language

Total Zambian Language Titles=248
Total English Titles=502

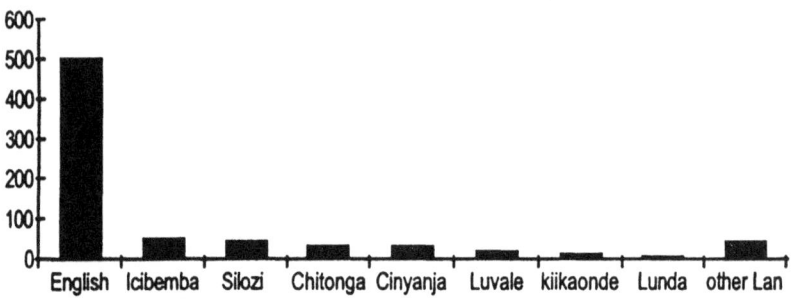

Appendix D
Categories of Stakeholders in the Book Industry

1. Publishers
2. Booksellers
3. Ministry of Education (Inspectors, Curriculum Specialists, Planners, etc.)
4. Booksellers and Publishers Association of Zambia
5. School Teachers
6. Donor Agencies funding the educational sector
7. Authors
8. Librarians

Appendix E
Distribution of Literacy in Zambia by Age Group

(a) **Population distribution:**
    Population age 5 + years   55.3%
    Urban population   71.4%
    Rural population   44.7%

(b) **Literacy by age grouping:**
    5–9 years   14.5%
    10–14 years   57.5%
    15–19 years   74.5%
    20–24 years   75.4%
    25–29 years   75.3%
    30–44 years   69.4%
    45 years and above   39.4%

Source: 1990 Census, Central Statistical Office, Lusaka, December 1990

6

Privatization of Publishing in the Côte d'Ivoire

ROBERT J. PALMERI

Just after gaining independence from France in 1960 the government of the Côte d'Ivoire[1] created a company, the Centre d'édition et distribution africaine (CÉDA) with the French textbook publisher Hatier as the other partner. The new company's initial purpose was to sell and distribute books from France and eventually begin publishing. In 1972 the Ivoirian government joined those of Senegal and Togo to create a multinational publishing house, the Nouvelles éditions africaines (NÉA), in which the governments together were the majority owners and a consortium of French publishers were the other shareholders. There were no other significant publishing houses.

Then in 1992 the government divested itself of majority ownership in NÉA. A new publishing house, Nouvelles éditions ivoiriennes (NÉI) was created in the process, with the French publisher Hachette as the majority owner. In 1996 the government sold more than half its share in CÉDA to the Ivoirian public. Now the Ivoirian government holds a minority share in the two companies. At first glance it appears to be a classic case of implementing the privatization process that has been an essential part of the structural adjustment programs imposed by the World Bank, the International Monetary Fund, and other economic assistance donors.

However, as one looks more carefully at the history of publishing in the Côte d'Ivoire, one realizes that the current status and future of the book and publishing industry is much more complex than meets the eye. The former colonial power, France, and the French publishing industry still play an extremely important role in the production and sale of books, not just in the Côte d'Ivoire but in all their former colonies in sub-Saharan Africa. Therefore, any study of publishing must look at the history of French-speaking Africa and its relationship with the former colonial power: France.

In order to govern its late nineteenth century African territorial conquests, France created two large colonial federations: French West

Africa and French Equatorial Africa. Although divided into fourteen territories, including one UN Trust territory in each federation added after World War I,[2] it was a highly centralized and hierarchical system managed from Paris with little room for local decision making. Economically, this colonial system had two primary goals. The first was the extraction and export of natural resources in their basic state to assist the industrial development of France. The second was the creation of captive markets for manufactured goods from France. No attention was given to the building of an industrial sector that would transform locally produced raw materials into final products for export.

Culturally, French colonial policy was to educate and acculturate a small elite, starting with the sons of traditional chiefs. These Africans were then employed in subordinate positions in the new colonial system. This *mission civilisatrice* was implemented through schools created by both the colonial administration and Catholic Church and were modeled after those in France. These schools prepared clerks, primary school teachers, and health care specialists (nurses and paramedics, the so-called "African doctors") to staff the lower levels of the administration. At the height of this system, Africans, who proved they had "evolved" by showing that they could speak and write French properly and had the cultural knowledge of a French person, were given a higher status. However, "evolved" Africans could never be quite equal to a French person, even when they had attended the same lycees as French children living in the colonies.

After World War II, the constitution of the Fourth Republic mandated that its colonies be brought closer politically to metropolitan France. As a result, the subjects of these African territories began electing deputies to the French National Assembly.[3] The original goal of this inclusion was to eliminate any independence movements from developing in the colonies. Territorial legislatures were also created to give Africans a limited role as "advisers" to the French colonial administrators. In 1958 Charles de Gaulle tried to develop a system that gave autonomy to the colonial territories within the context of a single French Union.

By the late 1950s the "winds of change" were blowing full gale through Africa and full sovereignty became the goal of all Africans. By this time the African deputies had become the poles of political activity in their territories, mobilizing many members of the African elite the French had created to help them make the colonial system run. However, the inability of these emerging African leaders to unite their political movements into a single force led to the dissolution of the two federations and the creation of many ministates when independence was granted in 1960.

These new ministates were ill-prepared for self-government and the French were asked to stay on. In the Côte d'Ivoire, the new president, Felix Houphouet-Boigny, strongly encouraged French involvement in the building of the new Ivoirian nation. The population of French nationals soared from about 11,000 at independence to more than 60,000 in the early 1980s at the height of the economic boom. This number has dwindled to approximately 25,000 in 1996—partially because of the growing number of qualified Ivoirians available but also because of the prolonged economic recession that lasted for more than a decade.

Since 1960 France has continued to base its position as a world power on the France-Africa axis that it has developed. Relations with African leaders are handled directly from the French presidency, and there is a biennial Franco-African summit. The French government also has a cultural policy based on the expanded use and propagation of the French language. This policy has included the creation of a French-speaking community of nations, "la Francophonie." While worldwide in scope, with strong participation of the French-speaking, parts of Canada and Belgium, this loose-knit community of nations is another tool for the French to keep French-speaking African nations within their political sphere by strengthening their ties to the French language. The operational tools of "la Francophonie" are a series of organizations to support educational and cultural activities. The most important of them is the Agence de cooperation culturelle et technique (ACCT), based in Paris.

Books and Publishing
Such a cultural and educational policy during the colonial period meant all publications and books could and did come from France. Even when some French publishers and the Catholic educational establishment began preparing materials adapted for African schools in the 1950s, they were written by French authors, then published and printed in France. Also, the first specific effort by French-speaking Africans to promote African culture and to publish the writing of Africans occurred

in Paris through la Société africaine de culture (SAC), founded by the Senegalese Alioune Diop after World War II. Closely allied with SAC was the journal Présence africaine and the publishing house of the same name. Continuing into the immediate post-independence era of the 1960s it was virtually the only place that a French-speaking African could have a creative work of literature published.

At this point it is useful to look at the nature of the book market in French-speaking Africa. Even during the colonial era the educational market, primarily textbooks, accounted for the lion's share of the books sold. That has changed very little over the years and today el-hi textbooks represent about 90 percent of the market in the Côte d'Ivoire. The figure is similar in all francophone African countries. To make a comparison with France itself, the textbook market there accounts for only 15 percent of the book market. Therefore, French textbook publishers have continued to protect and expand their position in this export market.

The Educational Market
In 1960 when the French sub-Saharan territories became sovereign nations much of the cohesion of the colonial system disappeared with the need for these countries to establish their sovereignty and individual personality. One priority was to expand educational opportunities for its citizens, each country doing so within its means. Nowhere in French-speaking Africa was this expansion more striking than in the Côte d'Ivoire. President Felix Houphouet-Boigny had a vision of a rapid development of both the economy and the educational system that would give his fellow Ivoirians a decent education and then ensure them a well-paying job. The result: in 1960 there were about 240,000 Ivoirians in primary school; in 1994–95 this number had increased sixfold to more than 1.5 million. At the secondary level there are now more than half a million students and more than 50,000 at the tertiary level.

In such a situation the growing need for textbooks meant that it would be natural for an indigenous publishing industry to develop in the 1960s and 1970s in the Côte d'Ivoire. However, nothing really happened until the 1980s, even though the Ivoirian government in conjunction with French publishers had created two publishing houses: CÉDA in 1961 and the Abidjan branch of NÉA in 1972 (later to become NÉI). However, CÉDA was in its early days primarily a book importer and distributor for books published in France. Even today about one-third of its gross revenues come from the sale of books it imports. In the 1980s these two companies finally became major publishers in their own right.

A protocol agreement signed in 1982 between the Ivoirian government and CÉDA and NÉA (Abidjan) gave the two companies the monopoly over the publication of textbooks for public primary schools. The textbook series, called Ecole et développement, was published initially between 1982 and 1988. Much of the series' editorial work was started in the 1970s, paid for by the French Ministry of Cooperation, and has involved French technical assistants as well as the work of Ivoirian educators. There are twenty-six books in the series, covering all subjects in the six years of primary school. The two publishers have an equal number of titles.

However, until 1994 almost all these books were printed in France. Even though there were several printers in the Côte d'Ivoire that were technically capable of printing the books, local costs were such that it was cheaper to print the books overseas and import them. In January, 1994 the CFA Franc was devalued by half, so the wholesale cost of imported goods doubled.[4] Since Ivoirian pupils must furnish their own textbooks, the government worked with CÉDA and NÉI to limit the inflationary effects of the devaluation by controlling the rise in textbooks prices. Part of the solution was to require the two publishers to print all primary school textbooks in the Côte d'Ivoire, where the costs were now competitive with foreign printers. As a result thirty-five years after independence from France a significant part of Ivoirian book consumption is finally being produced in the country.

The secondary school textbook market shows a very different face because very few books are published in the Côte d'Ivoire. However, virtually all the textbooks approved by the Ministry of National Education for use in public secondary schools are distributed by CÉDA and NÉI. The books are produced in France by French publishers and are either adaptations of already existing French textbooks or written by French authors for the francophone African market. In some cases the books are ostensibly copublished. There are even Ivoirian or other African authors, but often they are listed simply to make the book appear African. A case in point is the new textbook series for teaching English. Its publishers are listed as Macmillan (British), ÉDICEF (the Hachette subsidiary for publishing textbooks for Africa), and NÉI

(Ivoirian.) The series was originally written by a British ELT specialist who is listed as the lead author of the new Ivoirian version. Another Briton and three Ivoirians are coauthors. The last three all hold senior positions in the Ministry of Education, which give them a role in the textbooks selected for teaching English in Ivoirian secondary schools. Since virtually all these books are produced in France, pricing was a serious question after the 1994 devaluation. With the French Ministry of Cooperation, the French publishers concerned, NÉI and CÉDA, and the booksellers, the Ivoirian government was able to work out a price schedule that minimized price increases. The cost to the French government throughout the CFA zone has been very high, but it had to help French publishers preserve their markets, which would have otherwise shrunk drastically.

The previous discussion of the educational market has been limited to those books for public primary and secondary schools. However, there is a significant private school market as well. Most, including those run by the Catholic Church, follow the Ivoirian curriculum and therefore use the textbooks prescribed by the Ivoirian Ministry of Education, because the success of their students depends on exams organized by the ministry. Schools that prescribe other textbooks do so at their peril because success on the primary school leaving exam, the entrance exam into secondary school, and the graduation exams for the equivalent of junior and senior high school diplomas depends heavily on having used the "official" textbooks. The other textbooks that are available are either meant for the French curriculum (there are a number of schools at both the primary and secondary levels that are part of the French educational system) or were originally meant for Ivoirian schools but have not been updated for years and are no longer totally compatible with the Ivoirian school curriculum. The latter category are still available in many bookstores, particularly the small independents and the sidewalk vendors.

In the secondary school market there are two trends worth noting. The first involves CÉDA and NÉA/NÉI. In the 1980s they had started getting involved with their French partners and other textbook publishers in assuring the distribution of adaptations of French textbooks for the Ivoirian market. In the late 1980s, they started copublishing, although they were never the lead publisher (see earlier description of NÉI's English series.) In the last couple of years they have started publishing books that supplement the official textbook in a given course.

There are two types: workbooks in which the students write out exercises and collections of past exams with model answers and suggestions to help pass the external examinations. In these last cases both the financing and the editorial control come from in-house sources and do not involve French publishers.

The second trend involves the handful of local independent publishers that have come into being since 1990. All have started as trade publishers but as of early 1996 only one, Éditions du livres du sud (ÉDILIS), had published more than ten titles. In 1994 ÉDILIS made an important breakthrough in the secondary school textbook market. With the changes in the Ivoirian political system that took place in 1990, the civic education curriculum became irrelevant and incorrect. Working with the Ministry of Education, ÉDILIS has published four new textbooks in civic and moral education for junior high school. They hope to use this series as proof that they are a serious player in the textbook arena. They have also prepared a series of readers to teach literacy and vocational skills to illiterate women, in cooperation with the Ivoirian government.

More importantly, the new independent presses have made the point continually, both with the Ivoirian government and in public, that they can never establish a strong foundation without having a share of the textbook market. CÉDA and NÉI executives riposte that ending the monopoly agreement at the primary level will both bring an end to their companies and lower the quality of textbooks published in the country. Of course, the French publishers engaged in the African market prefer the status quo because they have a privileged position. But what about the Ivoirian government? Is it simply protecting its investments or does it really believe that in a small market like that of the Côte d'Ivoire, concentrating resources in two companies will result in better service?

Trade Publishing
Although textbooks make the profits for publishing in Africa, when one talks about publishing one is almost always referring to trade publishing: fiction and nonfiction. What is the situation in the Côte d'Ivoire? Once again, CÉDA and NÉI are the giants. Beginning in the late 1970s and through the 1980s, they published novels, short story and poetry collections, children's literature, the occasional play, and some nonfiction, particularly in the field of Ivoirian history. With the exception of

those works that became required reading in the schools, virtually none of these titles has sold very many copies.

One reason is that the Ivoirian public is not considered to be readers. Another is that neither CÉDA nor NÉA/NÉI have significant distribution capabilities outside the Côte d'Ivoire. Even during the era when NÉA was multinational, it was rare to find NÉA titles published in Abidjan available in Dakar or Lomé, or vice versa. Finally, neither publisher has spent any significant resources in promoting their trade titles. In fact in discussions with Ivoirian authors who have been published by the two giants the primary complaint is that neither do anything to promote the sales of their works.

Another factor that one must note when looking at trade publishing in French-speaking Africa was the creation in the 1970s and 1980s of several Africa-oriented publishers based in Paris following in the footsteps of Présence africain. The most important are l'Harmattan, Karthala, Sepia and Silex/Editions du sud, plus Hatier's Collection monde noir poche (modeled after Heinemann's African Writers Series and distributed in the Côte d'Ivoire by CÉDA). The lion's share of fiction by Africans or academic books about Africa written in French is published by these six houses and not in Africa. And the overwhelming majority of these books are published with subsidies of one sort or another: ranging from author's participation to grants that supported the author's research or writing of the work and included funds for its publication. Two of the most important funding sources are the French Ministry of Cooperation and ACCT.

As a result, these houses survive and even prosper on the up-front funding of their publications and not on the sales of the works. In fact, sales in Africa are very limited because their prices are so high. At a recent literary conference in Abidjan, an Ivoirian literature professor remarked to a visiting Senegalese author whose most recent novel is published by Harmattan that he had thought about buying the book, but when he saw it cost the same as a half sack of rice that would feed his family for more than a week, he decided against the purchase.

Naturally, authors start with those publishing houses that they think have the broadest reach and will do the best job in promoting and selling their work. This means approaching a French publisher in the first instance. There are two options: one is to try a general publishing house that has occasionally published African authors. The most sought after is Éditions du seuil, which publishes the late Congolese author Sony Labou Tansi and the Ivoirian author Ahmadou Kourouma.

The other is to go to one of the above publishers that concentrate on Africa.

Only after these avenues are exhausted do African authors return home to look for a publisher. In the Côte d'Ivoire they start with CÉDA and NÉI. By informal agreement imposed on them by the government, each publishes at its own expense about five new titles a year outside the textbook realm, a small price to pay for their privileged position in the most lucrative market. If both CÉDA and NÉI say no, then authors finally look to the local independent publishers.

Who are the new independent publishers? They are characterized by their national character, both in their ownership and the makeup of their personnel, their nongovernment ownership, their low level of production (one to four titles per year), and their lack of access to outside financing. Most are publishers of their own works, but several have concentrated on publishing the writing of others. In 1996, only three seem to be emerging from their modest beginnings. The first, ÉDILIS, is directed by a former NÉA staffer. In addition to being the only independent to break into the textbook market, it has published seven works of fiction since 1992 and created a backlist by taking over a number of previously published titles from NÉA, namely some children's literature and books promoting the learning of indigenous languages. The two others started as niche publishers: Éditions Neter as a scholarly publisher and Éditions juridiques as publisher of Ivoirian codes and laws. Éditions Neter has recently published several titles promoting the image and programs of Ivoirian President Henri Konan Bedié. As a consequence, it may eventually have access to financing that will allow it to expand its scholarly production or break into the textbook market. Two others which have concentrated on publishing the works of others have stagnated because they have not been able to get their sales to a level that will allow them to publish new works.

Privatization
The place of the two major Ivoirian publishers has been discussed within the context of the entire industry. Now let us look at the ownership history of each one.
Centre d'édition et distribution africaine (CÉDA): The Centre d'édition et de diffusion africaine, commonly known as CÉDA, was created in 1961 by the Ivoirian government with the French textbook publisher, Hatier. The purpose of the new company, as indicated in its name, was

to become both a publisher and distributor of books. It also had regional pretensions, preferring to call itself African rather than just Ivoirian, which was the case with most other companies in which the government was involved. As discussed earlier, for the first twenty years of its existence it was primarily a book distributor and did not get into serious textbook publishing until the early 1980s.

With a modest capital base of 2,000,000 CFA (U.S.$8,000) in 1961, the Ivoirian government held only a 25 percent share. Hatier held the remaining capital and effectively controlled the company. Over the next thirty years, the capital increased and the shares held by government changed. The Ivoirian government increased its share to 51 percent in 1974, to 60 percent in 1982. During this period there were also steady increases in CÉDA's capitalization—to 132,000,000 CFA by 1987.

In 1992, CÉDA had a major restructuring of its capital and effectively began the process of "privatization." The capital amount was increased by 350 percent—to 461,000,000 CFA. Also the Canadian publisher HMH Hurtubuise bought 9 percent of the company's capital, cutting back the Ivoirian government's share to 51 percent. But Hatier and HMH Hurtubuise were owned by different branches of the same family and were the only foreign publishers involved in the company, holding collectively 49 percent of CEDA's shares.

In the early 1990s the Ivoirian government began a process of disengagement from the economic sector, selling off all or a part of its shares in many parastatal corporations. In some cases, the government negotiated with interested parties the sale of its assets, effectively handing over control of the Ivoirian parastatal to another company—often French. In other cases, a certain percentage of the government's shares were offered for sale to the public through the Abidjan Stock Exchange.

For CÉDA the process went public in early 1996 when 31 percent of the company's shares, all held by the government, were offered for sale. The shares, having a face value of 5,000 CFA (approx. U.S.$10.00) were offered at 8,250 CFA (approx. U.S.$16.50.) There was not a great rush to buy up the shares as had happened with several other better known companies, but within two weeks of the official closing of the offer, all were sold. CÉDA's capital is now divided up as follows: Ivoirian government 20 percent; Éditions Hatier 40 percent; Éditions HMH Hurtubuise 9 percent; and publicly held 31 percent.

Although Hatier/Hurtubuise do not hold a majority of shares, they will perhaps have a stronger hand in the management of the company than they have had in the past without having changed their position within the company.

Another development that has taken place simultaneously is that the Hatier Group, the largest independent French textbook publisher, was bought by the megagroup Hachette, which is also majority owner of NÉI. The new owners have announced that they do not plan to change the editorial policies of Hatier. However, it remains to be seen how long such a policy will stay in place as Hachette managers rationalize the management and production of their several subsidiaries that are engaged in textbook publishing and, more importantly, their African investments.

Nouvelles Éditions Ivoiriennes
The other major publisher in the Côte d'Ivoire is the Nouvelles éditions ivoiriennes (NÉI), created in 1992 after the 1988 bankruptcy of the multinational Nouvelles éditions africaines (NÉA), which had been owned by the governments of Senegal, Côte d'Ivoire, and Togo. The publishing company was originally created in 1972 by then Senegalese president Leopold Senghor. Initially the Senegalese government held 20 percent of the capital, and a consortium of French publishers, which included major textbook publishers Armand Colin, Nathan, and Hachette, held the remaining shares. Immediately thereafter the capital was increased and the ownership was opened to the other two governments, so that each government held 20 percent of the shares and the French publishers the remaining 40 percent.

Although NÉA was "multinational," its President-Director General was always a Senegalese and based in Dakar. However, the Abidjan and Lomé branches were quite independent of Dakar's supervision, making their own editorial and marketing decisions. Effectively, there were three publishing houses united by a single name. Those who knew the situation could tell which branch had published a given title by looking at the title page. If Dakar were listed as the first city under the publisher's name, then it was the Senegalese branch. If Abidjan came first, then the book had been published by the Ivoirian branch. Things began coming apart in the mid-1980s, when mounting debts began interfering with the ability of the company to stay afloat.

In 1988 the three governments agreed to split up the company, and each took over the assets and liabilities attributed to the NÉA branch in the host country. In Senegal the Dakar branch was relatively quickly "privatized." President Abdou Diouf arranged to have several Senegalese invest in a new company known as Nouvelles éditions africaines, Senegal (NÉAS). Even though its ownership had changed, very little else did. The former head of NÉA became the head of NÉAS, and there were few staff changes.

In the Côte d'Ivoire, the Abidjan branch was taken over by the government. In 1989 it created a temporary entity known as the "Bureau ivoirian des Nouvelles éditions africaines" (BINÉA) until it decided what to do with the company. The company was effectively in receivership. Few new titles were published and sales were down. In 1991 the government's Privatization Committee offered BINÉA up for sale. The new terms were to be 55 percent private ownership by an individual, company, or consortium deemed qualified to take over majority ownership of the company. The qualifications included both financial and publishing capabilities. Of the remaining 45 percent, 20 percent would remain in Ivoirian government hands and 25 percent will eventually be sold through a public offering similar to that by which shares in CÉDA were offered recently to the public.

There were at least two bidders and the government selected the Hachette Group, represented by its textbook subsidiary ÉDICEF and its Ivoirian publications distribution company, ÉDIPRESSE, to become the new majority owners. In 1992 the group created a new company, Nouvelles éditions ivoiriennes (NÉI). Although the chairmanship of the board of directors is always held by an Ivoirian, the chief operating officer is a career Hachette manager, up until now French. It is possible that in the future one of the Ivoirian staff will become the managing director but it does not appear probable.

Conclusion
Both large Ivoirian publishers have been privatized in a limited sense because the Ivoirian government still holds 20 percent ownership in CÉDA and 45 percent ownership in NÉI. However, France's Hachette Group has become the dominant force in Ivoirian publishing because it now owns 40 percent of CÉDA and 55 percent of NÉI. Hachette also owns the local publications distribution company, ÉDIPRESSE, which has a virtual monopoly on newspaper and magazine distribution as well as importing and distributing books published by the Hachette Group. The dominance of one foreign publisher in the Ivoirian book and publications industry means that privatization could spell disaster for attempts to promote the growth of indigenous publishing and diversity within the industry.

Since success in the textbook market will determine whether new publishers can expand into viable long-term entities, Ivoirian government policies concerning the adoption of new titles by publishers other than CÉDA and NÉI will be the most important determinant. If the Ministry of Education is slow to approve additional titles by other indigenous publishers at the secondary level and continues the monopoly accord at the primary level, there is very little chance that additional publishers will emerge.

In addition, the attitudes of the French publishing industry and the French government are also important. But, with the Hachette Group in such a predominant position, it remains to be seen if they will allow new competition to emerge with the support of the French government. The tendency of the French in their former colonies has been to promote monopoly arrangements within a particular sector so that a single or small group of French companies dominate. Therefore, other French publishers must be encouraged to work on joint ventures with Ivoirian or other French-speaking African publishers. These publishers would bring in needed technical expertise but also allow the African publishers some say in the running of the new ventures. In such cases the French government must be ready with financial support or guarantees to obtain bank loans in order for these new entities to have sufficient working capital to grow. The American experience supporting the growth of publishing in Mexico and Argentina as part of the 1960s Alliance for Progress is exactly what is needed now in places like the Côte d'Ivoire. American publishers set up joint ventures with indigenous Mexican and Argentinean publishers with USAID funding. Eventually the funding was reduced and the American publishers withdrew, leaving a more vigorous publishing industry in place.

Trade publishing has a different problem because its books are considered a luxury item in most households. It will only become profitable if more people start reading and buying books. The problem and its solutions are not unique to French-speaking Africa. Long-term reading campaigns for both students and the general public are essential. Libraries, both in schools and local culture centers, must be reinvigorated. Both require long-term funding commitments, either from the Ivoirian government or donors. Government guarantees to indigenous publishers to buy a certain number of copies of new titles to be placed in libraries would help reduce the risk factor, enabling publishers to issue more titles and perhaps get additional credit from commercial sources.

Selling prices of books must also come down. The government must eliminate taxes and levies on book production inputs to bring printing costs down. Publishers and booksellers must accept smaller margins and authors lower royalties. French publishers, particularly the Africa-oriented publishers, must do more co-publishing with African publishers, setting up a two- or three-tier pricing system that will allow books of interest to African readers to be sold at lower, affordable prices on the continent. Unfortunately, there are important French forces that are fighting against the effort to bring prices down. First, they believe lower prices for books from France demeans the value of French culture. Second, they believe the demand for books in Africa is price inelastic so that lowering prices will not encourage growth but simply reduce profits.

Finally the problem of intra-African trade in books must be surmounted. Francophone African publishers export very little of their production even to adjacent francophone countries. Transportation costs are high. Marketing budgets are non-existent. The importation of books from France dominates. The French government subsidizes transportation costs, removing that factor as a consideration. Sales representatives of major French publishers constantly visit Africa promoting their lists. The Ivoirian government and independent indigenous publishers must start emulating this approach. They must also try to set up joint ventures with emerging publishers in other countries. It will not be easy in the early days, but the long, hard battle to eliminate the effects of the balkanization of French-speaking Africa must begin sometime and somewhere. The recent creation of a new customs zone of those West African countries within the CFA zone should be the signal to publishers that their potential market goes well beyond the borders of the Côte d'Ivoire.

Notes

1. In the early 1980s the Ivoirian government decreed that the name of the country in English was the "Côte d'Ivoire" and no longer the Ivory Coast. In keeping with this change the noun/adjective "Ivorian" becomes "Ivoirian," although the former spelling is also acceptable.

2. French West Africa was made up of the territories: Mauritania, Senegal, Guinea, Soudan (now Mali), Upper Volta (now Burkina Faso), Côte d'Ivoire, Niger, Dahomey (now Benin), and Togo (which was a UN Trust Territory.)

French Equatorial Africa was made up of the territories of the Congo (not the Belgian Congo), Gabon, Ubangi-Chari (now the Central African Republic), Chad and Cameroon (which was a UN Trust Territory.)

3. Citizens of the so-called four communes: Dakar, Goree, Rufisque, and St. Louis (found in today's Senegal) had begun electing a deputy to the French National Assembly in the nineteenth century.

4. The CFA Franc is the common currency of twelve of the fourteen former territories of French West Africa and French Equatorial Africa. From 1946 until January 1994, it had a constant rate of exchange with the French franc: 50 CFA = 1 FFr and was freely convertible in international money markets. In January 1994, its value was cut by half, so that its new exchange rate has become 100 CFA = 1 FFr, effectively doubling the cost of imports.

7

Transition or Collapse? A Survey of the Prospects for Private Publishing in Central Asia

PERNILLE ASKERUD

In May 1996, I visited Turkmenistan, Uzbekistan, Kyrgyzstan, and Kazakhstan. Based on my impressions from this trip I will attempt to describe the current situation of the publishing sector in Central Asia with particular emphasis on the possibilities and difficulties facing private publishing enterprises. For the time being, very little private publishing is going on in these countries. As most publishing activities in Central Asia are initiated and funded by the state, this chapter will also describe the infrastructure that governs these activities.

State Monopoly

Despite strict censure of the contents of books published, Central Asia was rich by most standards during the Soviet era with a wide selection of quality books and magazines available at educational institutions, libraries, and bookshops. The vast majority of these books were in Russian. On an international scale, Soviet publishing was significant, producing about 10 percent of the titles published in the world annually. In addition, Russian was one of the four dominant languages for scholarly publishing in the world.

During the Soviet era, all publishing activities were governed from Moscow. As was the case with all other areas of industry, the production of books and other printed materials was centered in a few regional printing plants. The countries in Central Asia would develop and print a limited number of titles each year locally (primarily in indigenous languages) and there was also local publishing and printing capacity for newspapers. The publishing of locally produced titles in languages other than Russian increased during the 1980s, when publishing activities in Central Asia blossomed.

The provision of instructional materials to schools and other educational programs was an important element in the general system of book production and distribution. For all practical purposes, the flow of books to the education sector was free and abundant. All curriculum materials were designed, controlled, manufactured, and distributed (free of charge) by the state—as were pencils, classroom furniture, and teaching aids. The system ensured that all republics in the former Soviet Union had a uniform supply of curriculum materials and that the curriculum was the same.

Within this centralized monopoly system for book provision, the schools were free to select books and other learning materials they would like to have from a prescreened list of instructional materials; their selections then went through a series of approvals by the district educational authorities and the Ministry of Education. Cost considerations were seldom an issue, and in most cases the books eventually arrived as ordered, most of them from other Soviet republics. This was a "package approach." While the officials were expected to operate according to certain guidelines, it was not necessary for them to indicate priorities or provide economic analysis. As one government official expressed it, "We were like postmen."

Similar systems existed for the production of other titles and their distribution to bookshops and an extensive library system. There was, for instance, large-scale production of children's books, which contributed to the development of a high level of appreciation of books in children from an early age.

Just as there were state publishers specializing in textbooks and other instructional materials for different levels of education, so there were specialized state publishers for literature, for political, legal, socioeconomic, agricultural, artistic and cultural topics, for scientific and technical books and magazines, as well as dictionaries for indigenous languages. Most of these publishing houses still exist and many of them are said to have been privatized. How they survive and whether or not they are really in business are separate questions.

The Situation after Independence

Since independence, the situation has been very different. Like most of the former Soviet republics, the Central Asian countries are struggling to cope with the radical economic, political, and administrative changes taking place. The difficulties involved in establishing new forms of administration for a democratic system and in providing the framework to allow the development of a market economy are many and of bewildering diversity. Furthermore, the economic and social costs of restructuring have been far greater than anticipated. All of the countries in Central Asia have suffered from hyper-inflation and near total economic collapse.

The economic and political transition to an open economy has proven to be a complicated process that requires comprehensive reorientation, especially in terms of the legal framework for commercial transactions, in management structures, and in human resource development. It is a process that will take years to complete and it may be some time before conditions are more favorable for private publishing in these countries.

All industry sectors in Central Asia have been brought to their knees by the cessation of financial and other support from Russia and other former Soviet republics. A lack of foreign credit or sufficient hard currency make it almost impossible to import the necessary raw materials for book production from either Russia or other countries. This alone has brought about a near collapse of the publishing sector in the countries.

In spite of the centralized system, the previous setup for publishing maintained a certain level of publishing capacity, with skilled professionals in each country, which is a valuable resource for the development of private publishing. Due to the nature of the previous system, this capacity is, however, unevenly developed, and for more private publishing enterprises to develop, comprehensive human resource development in the areas of publishing management, manuscript development, electronic publishing, and promotion and sales is very much needed. In addition, much of the existing prepress and printing technology needs to be updated or replaced and professionals will need to develop new skills.

The book situation is probably the worst in Turkmenistan, which (as a policy decision) has ended all cooperation with Russia in this area. Consequently, the country has also stopped importing and selling Russian books. Turkmenistan has started printing most of their textbooks in Ukraine and Turkey as part of other business transactions. Business enterprises also have their printing done abroad, even small jobs like the printing of name cards. While this may make sense in the short term, it will ultimately only weaken the potential for the development of a national publishing capacity and eventual self-reliance.

Some figures from Kazakhstan can serve as an example for developments in the book sector in Central Asia during the last ten years. The 1980s were a growth period for the publishing houses with increased local publishing in vernacular languages—especially Kazakh, Korean, German, Uigurian, Russian, and Arabic. The books published in Kazakhstan were also produced for other republics in the region. (There is still, especially in the area of textbooks, a considerable barter trade in books to serve the linguistic minorities in each country.) During this decade, a total of 20,000 to 25,000 titles and about 40 million copies entered the book market in Kazakhstan every year. About 75 to 80 percent of this volume was produced in other Soviet republics, primarily Russia. In 1995, a total of 595 titles (or about 10 percent of the local production in previous years) were published in Kazakhstan; 112 of these titles were textbooks. The importation of new titles was similarly much less than before independence.

Apart from the titles that are sponsored by the government or semipublic institutions the other titles are mostly low-cost, popular literature with high print runs and immediate profit potential;[1] higher-quality publications produced at a private publisher's own initiative are few and far between. The situation is comparable in the other countries of Central Asia.

One of the new and most promising private publishers in Kazakhstan, Atamura (meaning "the heritage of our ancestors"), was established in 1992. The publishing house, which also publishes the newspaper *Gazeta Atamura*, has so far focused primarily on titles in higher education, although it aspires to publish titles with much broader appeal. From 1993–1995, Atamura published about thirteen titles (most of them in both Russian and Kazakh), including seven books concerning scientific methodologies, *A History of Kazakhstan* and *People's Pedagogy and Psychology*. It appears that many of these titles were produced with partial or full government funding. The publisher reports that these titles are in demand.

One of the former regional centers for Soviet publishing was in Bishkek, Kyrgyzstan, where the state printing house printed and distributed textbooks for use in all the schools in Central Asia. The manuscripts for these books came from Moscow but prepress production and printing were done in Bishkek. The facility is large and staffed with highly skilled personnel, although much of the equipment, especially for copy preparation, is very old. Though there are many manuscripts ready to be produced, this printing facility is now sadly underutilized—mainly due to a lack of operating capital. Since 1993, the printing house has only produced textbooks, funded primarily by external aid programs. Still, the total production (in 1994, thirteen titles; in 1995, twenty-seven titles; and in 1996, thirty-seven titles) represented only a fraction of its production capacity.[2] While private publishers are said to be working in Kyrgyzstan (one estimate is that there are about nine state publishers for each private publisher), no publications have been subcontracted to this major prinitng house at private publishers' expense.

Unfortunately, the information needed for a more thorough analysis of the publishing sector is scarce and, more often than not, difficult to use. Data provided on any topic by two different sources are frequently so divergent that estimates are rendered impossible. The impact, scale, and volume of private publishing is therefore perhaps best illustrated through what is available in the major bookshops and booksellers in the capital cities of Ashgabat, Tashkent, Bishkek, and Almaty.

As is to be expected in societies where education, reading, and books are highly valued traditionally, the booksellers are numerous and are found in the markets (among street stalls) and in regular shops. None of the bookshops, however, are of significant scale or volume. In Turkmenistan, since the importation of Russian books has been stopped, all the Russian titles for sale were imported before 1991. There is some trade in secondhand Russian books of all genres. The titles available in Turkmen (both in the old and the new alphabet) do not exceed fifty titles. Apart from some textbooks, they are predominantly books about the history and traditional culture of Turkmenistan, some titles authored by the president, Turkmen-language instruction (to introduce the new alphabet), and detective stories. With the exception of the detective stories, almost all of these titles are published with funding from the government or other semipublic sources.

This mix of genres for publishing in vernacular languages is repeated in the other countries. In the other Central Asian countries the selection of available titles is greater as they include Russian books. A great number of romance stories and many magazines are available— and, of course, a broad range of fiction and nonfiction Russian books, though the volume of these is far from what it used to be. This is not only due to difficulties in obtaining hard currency to pay for the Russian books but also a result of the deep crisis that has affected publishing in Russia and other countries in the Confederation of Independent

States since 1991.

There is definite market potential for books, especially in Russian, and specific demand for titles pertaining to business, management, computers, and foreign-language instruction. At the same time, there is also great interest in titles that relate to national identity, history, and culture. While there is no doubt that the appreciation of books and other printed materials in itself is sufficient to guarantee a market, the purchasing power of the population is affected by the economic crisis. While unbridled capitalism has made fortunes for a few, many people are now forced to live without the social safety net they were used to just a few years back, and without any means to overcome the problems of poverty. This has given rise to a rapid social and economic segregation in the countries that is reflected in the significant discrepancy between the impact of the transition in the countryside and urban centers (where the situation generally is much better). It also means that people, in general, have limited or no extra money to spend on books.

Privatization

In the countries we are discussing, many publishing and printing activities are said to have been privatized and there are varying degrees of competition between private publishers and state publishers. It should be noted that the new private publishers and printers are the same people who were working within the previous state publishing sector. There is great interest in starting new publishing businesses in all these countries. However, the conditions needed to create viable publishing businesses are not in place. Many of the publishing houses started since 1991 have therefore collapsed as illustrated in the example of Kazakhstan. While there are still fourteen state-owned specialized publishing houses, the National Agency for Information and Mass Media has over the last couple of years received 150 registrations for private publishing houses.[3] Of these only about 12 have survived, but the agency estimates that only 5 or 6 of these are actually working. It appears that conditions in Kyrgyzstan are currently the most conducive to private publishing enterprise.

There is no domestic or regional source in Central Asia for raw materials or printing technology; so all publishing and printing enterprises depend on the importation of these articles.[4] The private publishing houses all have a number of manuscripts ready for publishing, and most people in the business claim that a market for these books exists if they were to be published. However, many of the newly established private publishers cannot really function, primarily because they lack operating capital and access to the foreign currency or credit necessary to buy raw materials abroad. Production by private publishers in Central Asia in recent years, therefore, still depends on government (or other) funding.

In Central Asia private publishing houses are trying to establish themselves while the state or former state printing plants still maintain a limited monopoly on printing. In many cases, the printing houses appear to be more like parastatal enterprises. While this is probably due mainly to economic factors, it also means that government influence on what is in fact published is potentially quite considerable. The control over the supply of paper—which is at present extremely scarce—is another source of leverage for indirect and direct control over publishing.

The private publishing houses are generally quite small. The houses that publish newspapers seem to be the ones that survive. Many of these small publishers are also involved in advertising and information activities. While the old state publishing and printing houses all have problems obtaining the necessary funds to invest in new technology and to replace printing facilities, some of the newer publishing houses survive by competing on the strength of the quality produced by the new and more sophisticated technology. However, the scale of this activity is still very small.

The traditional approach to publishing still dictates (in spite of the dramatically different economic circumstances) the way the publishing industry is analyzed and conducted in Central Asia. The fact that management and work force remain essentially the same is a contributing factor to this situation. It is the most significant obstacle to the development of commercial publishing. The necessity for an adequate legal framework stipulating the rules and regulations pertaining to publishing activities with respect to the changed political and economic situation is not widely recognized; it is another serious obstacle to the further development of private publishing in Central Asia. National independence brought with it a need for national legislation and new management in all spheres of society. Such revisions, however, take time, and in all the countries appropriate legislative and regulatory frameworks are not yet in place. In many areas great uncertainty and confusion about the laws that govern a specific activity prevail, and this is certainly true for publishing activities. Similar difficulties pertain to management structures. The development of appropriate legislation and revised management structures is severely hampered by a lack of or an overly simplified understanding of exactly how private enterprise works and of the environment needed for it to develop and grow. Basic concepts of a market economy are often misunderstood. Hence much of the difficulty related to reliability of data and information is caused by the fact that the situation is still being analyzed on the basis of the old system. There is a great need for human resource development in public and private administration.

Finally, it is a serious problem for private publishing that no new infrastructure for the distribution of books has yet been fully developed. The existing system has only been slightly adjusted to the new situation; for the time being, there is simply no economically viable basis for a system to distribute books outside the cities. Kyrgyzstan is trying to do something about this through the newly established Association of Independent Book Distributors. Kyrgyzstan (the only country in Central Asia to do so) has also established a publishers association.

As shown above, government influence in the book sector is significant. In Turkmenistan and Uzbekistan there is still government control over what can and cannot be published. In these and the other countries, the administrative structure inherited from the old system still governs the environment for public publishing activities. The dominance of public funds in publishing gives the administrative structure power to dictate the terms for publishing activities. In practice, it forces private publishers to conduct business the same way that state publishers used to work.

The administrative structure centers around the former State Publishing Committee, which organizes the development, production, and distribution of many different kinds of publications. Previously, the different specialized publishing houses within this structure had a monopoly on publishing. Today, the committee can (in principle) subcontract to any public or private publishing and printing house. The state system also contains an organization responsible for distribution and a book chamber responsible for the approval of manuscripts and cataloguing, both of which are state funded. The committee is itself funded by the government.

The publishing industry still more or less revolves around this infrastructure. The committee negotiates funding for individual projects with the ministries. Once the books are published and delivered, the ministry allocates funds to another government unit, which in turn makes final payment to the publishing house or the committee directly. As an example, in Turkmenistan income from publishing is dispersed according to a fixed ratio with 60 percent going to the publisher, 10 percent to the printer, and 30 percent to the distributor. In economic terms, the state is acting as the main publisher, out-sourcing different parts of the production process to publishers, printers, and distributors. In such a system there are so many hidden subsidies and fixed costs that the unit cost does not necessarily reflect the real cost of production, nor does it really allow for competitive bidding. Further, in order to keep the cost of books as low as possible, the revenue has traditionally been set so low that it does not allow for overhead expenses such as investment in equipment (for which funding in the old system was always negotiated separately). Whether or not the private publishing houses working within this system can really be called private enterprises is debatable. It remains a fact that the current publishing scene is dominated by government-stimulated activities, notably textbook publishing and the news press. The dependence on foreign currency for the purchase of printing materials is another vehicle for indirect government influence. There is no doubt, however, that the principle of government monopoly has been abandoned.

The Book Sector

Of particular importance to an evaluation of the book sector is the high literacy rate and the high level of book appreciation in these countries. Central Asia is a region of literate societies. It is common to see people reading newspapers, magazines, and books in public. Another indicator of the level of book appreciation is the extensive and widely used library systems that were established during the Soviet era. It included a range of libraries from school and children's libraries to highly specialized research libraries. In Turkmenistan they had about 4,000 libraries for a population of less than four million people, while Kazakhstan used to have 20,000 libraries for a population of 16 million. Today many of these libraries are facing severe economic difficulties, and a number of libraries have been forced to close.

The National Library in each country is large, well stocked, and offers a wide range of activities. The National Library in Bishkek is the biggest library in the region and is still functioning very well despite economic difficulties. It can serve to illustrate the scope of these libraries. The library has a stock of about six million books. Of these 42,000 volumes are reference materials and handbooks; 160,000 are rare books or manuscripts. Every day between 500 and 1,000 users visit the seventeen reading halls. At the end of the academic semester these figures are considerably higher. Formerly, the national libraries automatically received copies of each book that was published in the Soviet Union. Provision of books to specialized libraries, district libraries, school libraries, etc. was likewise guaranteed. This system has, of course, collapsed now, and it has not been possible yet to acquire sufficient funding for the acquisition of new books through other means.

Textbooks and Other Instructional Materials

The situation in the book sector is, of course, greatly affected by developments in the education sector. Though the situation varies from country to country (and quite a lot from rural to urban areas, within countries), all the countries share difficulties in funding and maintaining their school systems. The economic problems are mounting, and simply keeping the schools open is becoming a problem in many areas. For the time being almost all school-age children are attending school (as required by law). However, as the cost of school supplies is increasingly being transferred to the parents, it is becoming more and more difficult to ensure that children attend school. A serious decline in the previously high quality of education is caused by a critical shortage of textbooks and other instructional materials in all the countries. While primary school pupils, especially in rural areas, lack such basic learning materials as workbooks, pens, and pencils, university students must to a great extent rely on libraries for the books they need and often study from books that are ten to fifteen years old.

Again, Kazakhstan can serve as an example for what is happening in the other countries. After independence in 1992, the Kazakh government provided special funding for the production of textbooks; this was followed by the initiation of a special support program in 1993. Economic developments and the rising costs of paper and other raw materials have, however, made it impossible for the government to provide sufficient funding to maintain this program. There have been no government funds allocated since June 1994, with the result that since September 1995 there has been no public provision of new books for children starting school, nor to any other group of students.

Under the previous system, the government book distributor in Kazakhstan, Kazakh Book, had 496 "shops" with an associated 12,000 outlets to serve the whole country, including remote villages in rural areas. Due to financial constraints there are only 140 of these bookshops left. Where these shops have closed, book distribution is left to private-sector publishing. Under current circumstances there is an inadequate economic basis for the development of a commercial distribution system for rural and remote areas. Another consequence of the diminishing government funding for school books is that the distribution and availability of books becomes uneven and that the rural population experiences a further depletion not only of school books, but of the general book supply compared to the cities. In the same manner, the Kazakhstan National Agency for Information and Mass Media has been forced to close down more than half of the libraries it was administering. Where there were about 20,000 libraries in the country before, there are now 8,000. It may only be a question of time before more will close.

The governments of Central Asia are all involved in negotiating loans and external aid which will be used to support their educational systems.

New Curriculum and Language Policies

All of the countries are in the process of comprehensive and ambitious curriculum reforms. New curricula have already been developed and put in place but many changes and adjustments will be necessary before these new curricula are established. In the meantime, new instructional materials are not always available. Teacher training programs need to be implemented on a comprehensive scale to change the teaching methodologies in use and ensure that the curriculum reform is, in fact, realized in the classrooms.

A significant policy change in this regard pertains to the linguistic situation in these countries. The Central Asian countries are multiethnic societies in which many languages are spoken. Formerly, Russian was the official language used in all the countries; vernacular languages were only taught sparingly and seldom used by educated people. Very few books were published in vernacular languages. Today, Russian is still the most widely used language, but the vernacular languages have become important to cultural and national identity.

The official language in Turkmenistan is now Turkmen; in Kazakhstan it is Kazakh; in Uzbekistan, Uzbek; while in Kyrgyzstan, both Kyrgyz and Russian are official languages. These languages and several of the other indigenous languages have now become official languages of instruction in school, while Russian and English are taught as foreign languages. However, many of the teachers do know these languages as well as they know Russian, and since it has not been possible to publish and distribute sufficient instructional materials in many of the vernacular languages, Russian still remains the primary language of instruction. The continued dependency on Russian book production for textbooks and other books means that the crisis that has hit the book sector in the rest of the former Soviet Union has great impact on book supply in Central Asia as well.[5]

The transition to national languages is complicated by other factors as well. Both Turkmen, Kazakh, Uzbek and Kyrgyz are Turkic languages. Turkmenistan (since 1994) and Uzbekistan (since 1996) have switched to the Latin alphabet for Turkmen and Uzbek instead of the Cyrillic alphabet formerly used. A similar change is also being considered by Kyrgyzstan and Kazakhstan. The change constitutes a return to the alphabet used earlier in this century and has a profound impact on the publishing industry.

In order to fulfill these new requirements, new instructional materials must be developed, produced, and distributed for all topics and all levels of schooling. Adequate supplementary reading materials in indigenous languages do not exist to support even basic education. Supplementary reading materials must thus also be developed. Although this is the plan, for the time being, the actual situation in schools and other educational institutions is characterized by a serious shortage of books or by textbooks that do not necessarily correspond with the new curriculum or educational policies. To achieve the policy goals for education in Central Asia, the publishing sectors are in serious need of support and development. All the countries are under considerable external pressure to involve private publishers in the production of new materials instead of relying on the existing state infrastructure.

Conclusion
The main problems facing the publishing industries are shared by all the countries of Central Asia and are summarized as follows:

Identification of market potential:
- What is the market for the publishing industry? The transition to a market-driven economy calls for a different market structure and requires the publishing industries to identify market potential under these new circumstances. A serious obstacle for the publishing industry is that the kind of information needed to evaluate the market and develop business projections is simply not available at present. The situation is, of course, not helped by the doubtful quality of the information that is available, and by the general absence of a framework for analysis that reflects the parameters of a market economy.[6]
- The publishing industry is always influenced by government spending on book provision to the education sector; the uncertainty surrounding government's ability to continue financing book provision creates significant uncertainty in the market.

No definite legislative structure for book related activities:
- Financial instability and the fact that there is no definite regulatory framework for book production make it very difficult to do business projections or to attract investors or justify investments.

Absence of industrial and professional network:
- The publishing industries formerly relied on a network of suppliers, distributors, and publishing professionals within the Soviet Union. Since this network has more or less collapsed there is a great need to establish alternative relations and connections. Participation in international organizations and networking on a person to person, institution to institution, and publisher to publisher basis, could provide a tremendous opening and simulate the initiative and capacity that exists in these countries.
- There is, similarly, a great need and demand for international contacts and communication in other areas of the book sector, such as libraries and author's associations. All the countries of Central Asia suffer from profound isolation. They have little exposure or access to new ideas or alternative ways of doing things. In publishing, they lack contact with international associations and networks though they ex-

press a very keen interest in making such contacts. Nor have they participated in international book fairs or exhibitions. The import and export of books and other printed materials are at present inconsiderable. Language may be a problem in this connection as many people in Central Asia do not speak international languages other than Russian.
- Emigration is another factor in the collapse of existing professional networks. Central Asia has experienced a high level of emigration of people who had been forcefully moved here. Many skilled professionals, also from the publishing sector, have left.

Lack of access to raw materials:
- With insufficient access to foreign currency it has become almost impossible to import paper and other raw materials needed by the publishing industry. The Central Asian countries used to import all their paper from other Soviet republics; several initiatives are considering the possibilities of starting domestic or sub-regional production of paper and ink. Access to paper, cardboard, ink, and various chemicals needed for plate making is generally considered the biggest problem facing the publishing industries in Central Asia.

Insufficient human resources and technology:
- The radical change in the parameters for planning and management necessitates the development of new skills in analyzing and managing publishing enterprises. Training in skills related to publishing management, promotion, and sales is very much needed.
- Due to the previous system, the publishing capacity is unevenly developed. There is a specific need for professional training in areas such as manuscript development and electronic publishing.
- In addition, there is a need to update equipment and the corresponding skills of the publishing professionals and to ensure maintenance of printing facilities

When asked, people connected to the book sector in Turkmenistan, Uzbekistan, Kyrgyzstan, and Kazakhstan with a near unified voice identify finding sufficient operating capital and access to foreign credit as key to improving the current situation. However, solving this problem alone might allow the continuation of "business as usual" and does not take account of the fundamental societal and economic changes taking place. It is the stated goal of all these countries to become open economies. When this happens the publishing sector will be exposed to international competition. If the publishing industries are to survive under these new conditions a thorough reorganization is needed. Good management is, without a doubt, as essential as financing to the development of publishing capacity into commercially viable national publishing industries.

To support the transition there is a need for a regulatory and legislative framework that promotes publishing and creates the conditions that makes it possible for commercial publishing industries to develop and survive. The implementation of commercially oriented management strategies at the level of individual publishing and printing houses is needed to confront a still-undeveloped market economy and to provide appropriate solutions to the many new problems that will arise. Ultimately, the problem of securing credit and raw materials must be solved through appropriate management strategies. The issue of management is a very sensitive one. The management function of a command economy differs from that of a market economy where performance is measured by the economical success of the company and not only by how well production targets are met. The new set of skills required will necessitate comprehensive human resource development programs.

The transfer of skills and technology is often undertaken in connection with joint ventures. As in all other areas of business there is great interest in this and other forms of cooperation with international publishers. However, as long as the conditions under which such publishing activities are to be undertaken remain as unclear, it is unlikely that the publishing industry can attract much interest from abroad. It would strengthen the business potential of the industry if all the countries were to clarify the legal and regulatory framework for the publishing industry and encourage foreign investment by (for instance) giving the publishing industry priority status.

Such a review should also clarify the position taken vis-à-vis international agreements such as the Universal Copyright Convention and trade conventions such as the Florence Agreement. None of the countries have ratified any of these international agreements. One example of the need for re-organization is thus illustrated in the fact that the majority, if not all, of the publishers are said to obtain ISBN numbers for their publications from Moscow.

Kyrgyzstan has developed a draft law concerning publishing activities in the Kyrgyz Republic, and the National Agency for Information and Mass Media of Kazakhstan has, likewise, developed and proposed a plan to develop a more supportive policy environment for the book sector.[7] In both cases, these proposals are awaiting government attention and consideration. Turkmenistan and Uzbekistan are also said to have developed similar legislation.

In conclusion it can be said that though the countries recognize that the development of the book sector is an important element in the development of the countries' self-reliance, this recognition has yet to gain expression through the creation of a consistent policy environment that favors the development of an independent publishing industry. By defining the rules, regulations, incentives, and restrictions that apply to book production and book distribution, the formulation of such national book policies hold the potential for achieving the transformation of the book industry in Central Asia. To be effective, however, it is absolutely necessary that such legislation is based on a rigorous analysis of the current situation and a clear view of what is needed for the book sector to develop during and after the transition to an open economy. At present the data needed for such analyses are not available.

In addition, it is vital to ensure free access to printing resources, notably paper and printing capacity, whether this access is in effect controlled directly through ownership or by indirect means such as, for example, currency regulations.

It is important to keep in mind that the present situation in Central Asia is a direct consequence of the radical transformation of the larger society that is taking place. It has resulted in a situation similar to the situation of many low-income, developing countries. However, the current combination of human resources and infrastructure now in place in Central Asia differs radically from that of many developing countries. In some respects, the present situation has more similarities to the disruption caused by war. To avoid the disappearance of the skilled human resources that are available for the development of private publishing, there is an urgent need to deal with all of the abovementioned issues and not to resort to a strategy based on a superficial analysis of the most apparent problems of the transition process.

Notes

1. It is interesting to note that many publishers do not count these types of publications, and thus they are not reflected in their statistics.

2. The increase in production shown in these figures is entirely due to earmarked funding for school books provided to Kyrgyzstan by DANIDA. These funds have now been exhausted.

3. This agency was formerly the Ministry of Information and Mass Media.

4. Several initiatives to start local paper manufacture and production of other raw materials needed for printing are presently being considered in the countries of Central Asia, but serious projects have yet to materialize.

5. "In Russia, supplies of books declined by 10% between 1989 and 1990, by 17% in 1991, and by 16% in 1992. The number of textbook titles produced in 1992 was half the number available in 1984. That the decline comes at a time when many curriculum materials have been discarded in Russia also and need to be replaced by new materials only aggravates the situation." (Source: *Russia—Education in Transition*. The World Bank/ECA Country Dept. III/Human Resources Division [Washington, D.C. : World Bank, n.d.].)

6. The difficulties in obtaining accurate information also effects this preliminary survey of the book sector in these countries. The information provided in this article is to the best of my knowledge correct, but it is not very exhaustive.

7. Unfortunately, I have not been able to study these documents yet so I cannot at present comment on their contents and potential effectiveness.

CONTRIBUTORS

Philip G. Altbach is director of the Research and Information Center of the Bellagio Publishing Network. He is also professor of higher education at Boston College. He is editor of *Publishing and Development in the Third World*, co-editor of *International Book Publishing: An Encyclopedia*, and other books.

Pernille Askerud has worked as publications officer for UNESCO's Regional Office for Education in Bangkok, and is currently consultant to UNESCO, the Education for All Forum, and others. She is a graduate of the University of Copenhagen.

Paul Brickhill was executive secretary of the African Publishers' Network (APNET). Prior to that, he was involved in publishing in Zimbabwe. He is currently working on a UNESCO-sponsored publishing project based in Zimbabwe.

Richard A. B. Crabbe is General Manager of Africa Christian Press, Ghana. He is President of the Ghana Book Publishers Association and Board Member/Treasurer of the African Publishers' Network (APNET). Crabbe is also a board member of Media Associates International, USA. His main professional interests are strategic planning, editing, and training.

Ray Munamwimbu was born on January 14, 1957 in Monze district, Zambia. He obtained a Bachelor of Arts degree in education with merit from the University of Zambia in 1980, and for several years taught school. In 1984, he joined the then Kenneth Kaunda Foundation (now Zambia Educational Publishing House) as an editor in the English section. He became publishing manager in 1991. In November 1995 he was appointed marketing manager in the same organization. He is the current chairman of the Booksellers and Publishers Association of Zambia.

Robert J. Palmeri lives in Abidjan, Côte d'Ivoire, where he is engaged in a variety of activities promoting educational and cultural exchanges between West Africa and North America, including the movement of literature and knowledge through books, periodicals, and electronic means. He was formerly director of Book Programs at the U.S. Information Agency. He also directed USIA's Paris-based Africa Regional

Services, which provides a variety of written materials from the United States, translated into French for use by American Cultural Centers in Africa. Among these are the series Nouveaux Horizons, a collection of American books for distribution in French-speaking Africa.

Atnafu Wassie is a publishing expert who has served as curriculum and textbook expert in the Institute for Curriculum Develpment and Research and as head and acting manager of the editorial division and textbook publishing department, respectively, of the Educational Materials Production and Distribution Agency of the Ministry of Education in Ethiopia.

www.ingramcontent.com/pod-product-compliance
Lightning Source LLC
Chambersburg PA
CBHW070629300426
44113CB00010B/1714